D0983776

AMERICA AT LAST

By the Same Author

THE SWORD IN THE STONE

THE WITCH IN THE WOOD

THE ILL-MADE KNIGHT

ENGLAND HAVE MY BONES

BURKE'S STEERAGE

THE AGE OF SCANDAL

THE SCANDALMONGER

THE GOSHAWK

THE ELEPHANT AND THE KANGAROO

MISTRESS MASHAM'S REPOSE

THE MASTER

THE BOOK OF BEASTS
A translation of a Latin Bestiary of the twelfth century

THE ONCE AND FUTURE KING

THE GODSTONE AND THE BLACKYMOR

FAREWELL VICTORIA

America At Last

THE AMERICAN JOURNAL OF

T. H. WHITE

WITH AN INTRODUCTION BY

DAVID GARNETT

G. P. Putnam's Sons New York

Published simultaneously in the Dominion of Canada by Longmans Canada Limited, Toronto.

Library of Congress Catalog
Card Number: 65-18474

PRINTED IN THE UNITED STATES OF AMERICA

INTRODUCTION

In January 1964 my friend Terence Hanbury White was found dead in the cabin of the liner which had brought him during the night to Athens. He was on a cruise to Greece after a lecture tour in the United States during which he had kept this journal. Tim is best known as the author of *Mistress Masham's Repose* and of *The Once and Future King,* a re-interpretation of the cycle of legends centered around King Arthur, first collected in English by Sir Thomas Mallory about five hundred years ago. Mallory had inspired Tennyson to write *The Idylls of the King,* William Morris to write *The Defense of Guinevere* and Mark Twain to write *A Yankee at the Court of King Arthur,* before he inspired Tim, and he will undoubtedly be the source of many other versions in the future. Some readers of this book will only know of *The Once And Future King* because it is the book from which Loewe and Lerner concocted the musical *Camelot* in which Julie Andrews took the part of Guinevere and Richard Burton played King Arthur. Others will only have read the first part, published separately under the title *The Sword in the Stone.*

When I first met him, and during the years when I saw most of him, Tim was a magnificent man physically. He was about six foot two in height with brilliant blue, always bloodshot, eyes, a dark beard bristling in all directions like a thornbush and dark hair. He was formidable. In his later years his hair and beard turned gray and he grew fat, which may have been connected with a sluggish circulation from which he suffered. At first I accepted Tim at his face value. Early in our friendship he asked me for a book to read about Sir Walter Raleigh—he planned to write a play about him—and he said he only wanted to get the history right. "The fellow's character I understand already: it is my own." I thought it probable he really was like Raleigh. But he wasn't.

When he first introduced himself to me in 1934, Tim was a schoolmaster at Stowe School, who kept all sorts of different animals: snakes, badgers, fox cubs, hedgehogs, owls and hawks as well as a beautiful Irish red setter bitch called Brownie which was the creature he most loved during his life. He had written several books including a novel published under a pseudonym. He was anxious to give up schoolmastering and devote all his time to writing. After reading his book *England Have My Bones,* I encouraged him to do this. He was crazy about all blood sports—all of which he eventually gave up. We went together on various fishing expeditions and I once went out trying to shoot wild geese with him.

In one of the lectures he gave during the tour when he was writing this diary, he explained that when he was a small boy his parents separated and his home and education collapsed about his ears. "Everything collapsed at a critical time in my life and ever since I have been arming myself against disaster. In case, in the next disaster that jumps upon me, to be ready with defense. That is why I learn. . . . It is this sense of danger that makes me do the fantastic things that I have always done all my life. I have had to be good at everything."

And Tim went on to give his audience a list of his accomplishments: he could shoot with a bow and arrow, ride a horse, fly an airplane, train falcons, dive in an old-fashioned diver's suit, sail a boat, fish, shoot, drive fast cars, paint pictures, do carpentering, build houses with concrete, read medieval Latin and had taken first class honors at the University.

Much of this was true. Often his enthusiasm waned before he became expert and in some skills he remained a hopeless amateur. He fished for years of his life and talked and wrote continually about fishing and we fished together a good deal, but I would not say he was a really good fisherman. He was a hopelessly bad carpenter: the bookshelves he put up in my Yorkshire cottage looked as though they had been made by a woman who had never handled a hammer or a saw in her life and who had little idea what a shelf full of books weighed. He prided himself on training gundogs but they were not steady or obedient. On the other hand I went out with him with his Peregrine falcon Cressida after grouse on a moor in Ireland. There were only about half a dozen coveys of grouse in an area of about ten square miles and that day, though we put up one covey, we didn't get any because the falcon didn't see them. But a day or two afterwards my young sons went out with him and Cressida killed two grouse and my wife made grouse pie of them. He handled his falcon with great skill. Curiously enough he was much more modest about training falcons and hawking, than about the things he was not really good at. It is not the list of accomplishments that Tim boasted about which is revealing, but his sense of impending disaster, which drove him on to do them. There are two kinds of brave men: those who are fearless and those who feel fear and force themselves to overcome it. Tim belonged to the second class. I think that fear helped him to be a good writer: it quickened his sensibilities.

What made him particularly delightful as a companion was his mixture of eager enthusiasm and his sense of humor and of himself as a comic character. Moreover he and I shared a great many interests, besides shooting and fishing and a love of animals and their psychology.

I invited him to join me and my first wife in Ireland for a fortnight's fishing in February 1939. When we left he stayed on as a lodger in a small farm near Trim where my wife had found rooms for him while we were fishing for salmon in the river Boyne. He lived on there through most of the war years, occasionally going over the wildest part of Connaught to fly his falcons or to shoot geese, or to investigate the legends connected with the island of Inishkea.

It was during the war years, in Ireland, that he did much of his best work, writing and rewriting the volumes of the Arthurian cycle, and writing also the two fantasies: *Mistress Masham's Repose* and *The Elephant and the Kangaroo,* and also *The Godstone and the Blackymor,* the record of his personal experiences in Connaught. I think it is the best book about the Irish since the stories by Somerville and Ross.

Tim had had T.B. and he might not have been accepted for the armed forces. During those lonely five years he corresponded continually with me.

I had gone into the R.A.F. Intelligence at the Air Ministry. Tim wanted me to get him a job, saying that if I could not find him something in which he could use his brains, he would become a ferry pilot, or a sea cook, or man a gun on a merchant vessel. He was not qualified for any of these occupations and no one would have taken him on at any of them.

Tim's father, who was I believe a police superintendent in India, had been born in Ireland and for that reason Tim, later on in the war, imagined that he was of Irish nationality, began to learn Gaelic and used to write to me about "your" Government and "your" war. At one time he almost became a Roman Catholic, but he shied away from it at the last moment. But by the end of the war his Irish enthusiasms had waned.

He was very short of money in the war years, which helped to make him lead a regular life and was good for his work. He could not afford to drink as much Irish whiskey or brandy as he did later on, when he became rich. He was a bout drinker like the cowboys of the West and the Canadian lumbermen. That is, he would drink heavily for a week or two, then pull up and go for a time on the wagon. If there was what he felt to be a compelling reason, he would not drink at all. During the lecture tour he made of the United States while he was writing this diary, the young sister of his friend Tony Walton was his secretary who made all the arrangements for the tour. In order not to put her in an impossible position, he drank no liquor during the whole trip. Directly it was over he started drinking on the cruise to Greece and by doing so helped to bring about his death.

Soon after the war he came back to England and I lent him a cottage high up on the edge of the moor above Swaledale in Yorkshire where he spent an uncomfortable winter.

England was being strictly rationed by the Labour Government and he must have found it hard to feed himself and two large dogs and to keep the little cottage warm. I sent him parcels of vegetables and a few unrationed luxuries from time to time. The Swaledale people are kind and generous and helped him out. He had practically no money then.

In the early summer of 1946 he heard that *Mistress Masham's Repose* had been chosen as Book of the Month and he received a large capital sum from the United States. On my advice he went to live in the Channel Islands, where the rate of income tax is very much less than in England. He bought a house in Alderney and settled there, but the books he wrote there are trifling compared with those of the lean years. From then onwards he prospered financially and the choice of *The Once and Future King* as the book on which *Camelot* is based made him a rich man. He went to New York to assist in the rehearsals and his attitude to the production was extraordinarily sane and clear-sighted and quite unlike that which he often took with his publishers. He said to me when I met him just after his return:

"I realized that *Camelot* had only the faintest relationship with my book. It was something created by other people, with other objects in view. But they were going to pay me a lot of money, so that the least I could do was to be as nice to them as I could. So instead of criticizing *Camelot,* I agreed with everything they said and suggested. As a result they thought I was the most intelligent author they had ever come across and I enjoyed the whole thing immensely."

The visit was important to him in other ways as it won him a number of friends, the chief of which were Tony Walton the scenic designer and Julie Andrews his wife. Another warm friend was Richard Burton.

But Tim sought out other more unusual friendships than those with stars of the stage, or the screen, and the unique, lovable and extraordinary character of the man is revealed in his description of one of them in a letter written to me in September 1956.

"Some time last winter I began to think about people who were stone deaf and stone blind, as I suppose most people have occasionally thought, but most people dismiss the thought quickly on the grounds they have enough on their own plates already. There is room on my plate . . . so I wrote offering to entertain four deaf blinds on a week's holiday each per annum." The first of his afflicted visitors was a little elderly woman who had been deaf and blind since she was fourteen. Tim had taught himself to talk on his fingers and had interested some children in doing the same. Between them they taught "Puck" to swim, took her out in a boat and made her catch four fish. They helped her to run on the sands and she climbed to the top of the lighthouse.

The friendship that resulted went adrift eventually, but how many other men would have had the imagination, the tenderness and the courage to have embarked upon it?

One of Tim's limitations was that his outlook on the relations between men and women was that of an earlier age—of someone like Thackeray. Women for him were either tantalizing bitches who loved to ruin a good man, or else darling old nannies who would knit him stockings and to whom he could turn when exhausted by field sports or debauchery. Occasionally a great and good woman appeared whom he could idealize: such a one was my first wife Ray; such, later on, was Julie Andrews. This Victorian outlook makes his judgments about women boring. Luckily he did not go in for them very much, but the hated figure of his mother, the Witch in the Wood, was always likely to turn up.

In this conventionality—and in other ways—Tim resembled Kipling. Both were born in India, and came back to spend miserable lonely boyhoods dominated by fear. Both suffered brutal treatment at school. In both there was a touch of vulgarity that sometimes mars their work. Both had a streak of sadism. Both were at their best in writing about primitive people and animals in human terms. Both had a nostalgic longing for a wholly imaginary past.

It was not Tim's exact description of how to do things—though he did that well—which makes his books so delightful. It is his sense of humor, his gift for writing farce, his awareness of himself as a figure of fun—and of human absurdity in general. He was a master of slapstick humor and his books contain situations which ought to have been exploited by Chaplin or the Marx brothers on the screen. For example, the two Irishmen in *The Elephant and the Kangaroo* who get fastened together, back to back, by a cast of salmon flies in the back of their jackets and lose their tempers while trying to separate, but can't reach to hit each other. But this slapstick humor almost always is a means for revealing the characters of its victims. The fantasy setting of *The Elephant and the Kangaroo* enabled Tim to tell us all about the hopeless shiftless couple with whom he lodged during the war years, his exasperation with them and his tender love for them. The ridiculous situations between them and their lodger enabled him to show us all three, not simply as comic grotesques (himself as comic as they are) but with psychological truth and understanding.

Again in the early part of *The Once and Future King,* Tim is not only weaving a delightfully amusing story of knights errant riding about on absurd quests; he also initiates the reader into all the details of day-to-day life in a Norman castle, he reveals what it is like to fly through the night accompanied by an owl, to swim as a small fish in the moat, to stand sentry all through the night as one of them among the crazy and sadistic falcons.

The test of a writer is to enlarge the experience of his readers. Tim passes this triumphantly. He has also a message for us. Walt Whitman wrote:

> I think I could turn and live with animals
> They are so placid and so self-contained.
> I stand and look at them sometimes half the day long.
> They do not sweat and whine about their condition,
> They do not lie awake in the dark and weep for their sins,
> They do not make me sick discussing their duty to God,
> Not one is dissatisfied, not one is demented with the mania
> of owning things,
> Not one kneels to another, nor to his kind that lived thousands
> of years ago,
> Not one is respectable or industrious over the whole earth.
> So they show their relations to me, and I accept them,
> They bring me tokens of myself, they evince them plainly in
> their possession.

Tim's message is much the same. This diary of his travels across the United States was written without any thought of publication—he had the lifelong habit of keeping journals. Sometimes he is superficial; sometimes he is unfair. For example, his very funny discursion on fig leaves would not have been worded as it is if he had seen the glorious group of statuary by Carl Milles opposite the railway station at St. Louis. But even if they irritate, his judgments will induce reflection. Tim never forgot, when he was judging men, the organization of the warring ants which he loathed and the wonderful freedom of the flocks of wild geese which he loved as though they were his own people.

It is this mixture of wisdom and simplicity, together with a delight in the texture of all the things on earth, which makes Tim such an excellent writer, excellent for the boys and girls he loved to teach, excellent for us all.

David Garnett

AMERICA AT LAST

17 · 9 · 63

I WENT to America once before, and that was to stay with Julie Andrews when she was acting in *Camelot*, the musical. I was there two or three months and adored everybody, from Julie and Richard Burton to the affable stagehands, and I thought New York was stunning—not terrible, as expected. The result was that people liked me back.

The two things that appealed most to me about New York were the Queensborough Bridge and the comicality of the skyscrapers. The bridge, with its traffic as ceaseless as hell, was the sort of Colossus which Gustave Doré might have imagined—London Bridge in a way, but with elephantiasis, an enormity of grandeur, of sheer size that could not fail to be impressive. You expected to see King Kong swinging about among the girders.

The skyscrapers (I suffer from the horror of height called acrophobia) were more than huge building blocks to overhang and terrify you. They had taken pains to be cheerful or individual or artistic and, what is more, their owners had been willing to spend money on the decoration. The only part of a skyscraper that can afford to be different from its neighbors is its top. The rest has to be utilitarian. So the tops have a gaiety of their own. I can't help thinking that it is a good thing when even businessmen are ready to acknowledge beauty, whatever their idea of it may be, by ornamenting their structures with gargoyles that must weigh hundreds of tons and cost thousands of dollars. "Look at me," says one skyscraper, "pretending to be something to do with Santa Sofia." "Or me," says another, "I am Gothic, as you can see by my sort of perpendicular arches." In a way it is a funny charade, like a lot of huge square ladies trying on Paris hats. My favorite one—and you do get to have favorites—had an airy gilt crown (can it have been gilded, or has my memory deceived me?) which she illuminated at night, coquettishly.

And, of course, the night-lit cliffs of Manhattan, those sky-filling hugenesses of bright windows for troglodytes, were a wonder of the world—as was the sinister landscape of Central Park as you looked down on it after sunset. In it, I privately believed, there emerged during the hours of darkness prehistoric tribes of Cherokees, hidden underground during the daytime, to mingle with the bums, porces and queers.

What I didn't like about the American trip was the Boeing 707s. In these horrifying monsters I flew at incalculable altitudes with Julie's husband, Tony Walton, both of us with streaming colds, aching ears, pocketfuls of pills, and a gradually disintegrating carboard model of one of Tony's stage sets, unwrapped.

So this time we are going by sea in the *Queen Elizabeth.*

It is for a lecture tour which will cover the continent and probably destroy us with exhaustion—it is practically a matter of one-night stands. Julie's eighteen-year-old sister-in-law Carol is coming as my secretary, but really as a protectress. We are quarreling already about tickets, visas and lecture notes ("This is beginning to get me down" says Carol, when I point out that the notes won't be ready, which they won't—she then proceeds to invite a girl friend to tea) but this is a healthy attitude, and a safety-valve, and we can't permanently annoy each other after being friends for four years.

Our good relations, which are bound to be strained by three months of strenuous tour, depend on me. Carol I know to be an adorable member of an adorable family—not one bad one in the whole boiling—so anything which goes wrong will be my fault. I am a testy, opinionated old gentleman and in moments of stress I had better read this paragraph, preferably in private and on my knees.

It is best to face the fact, from the start, that we shan't make any money to bring back. For one thing we are going first class, and for another I have hotel bills and air fares to pay and Carol's wages—well worth it, in exchange for sanity and protection.

I am making the trip to distract the private unhappiness of old age, rather like knocking your head against a wall when you have toothache.

But today, coming down from London by train after a tussle with the American Embassy about visas, I suddenly realized that I might enjoy it—that we both might.

So why not write a book as we go? It would keep us observant, not be too much trouble for a short entry every day, and at least it could do no harm. Also, it would be a distraction in all those hundreds and thousands of miles by terrifying airplanes.

QUERY: Does it do harm to write needless books? "Of the making of books there is no end." Why write if you have nothing to write about? Is one trip round America sufficient excuse? Millions do it.

I suppose it is excusable, if you keep your eyes wide open.

18 · 9 · 63

One thing I had better remember is that Carol, like Tony, likes doing or saying the opposite. If I say, "You could write your own version in the book in red ink," she will (and did) reply, "Why red? It is my unfavorite color." The proper way to handle this type of conversation is to reply, "Very well, use green." Carol then answers, "I prefer red."

It takes longer, but it passes the time, and I suppose you do get there in the end.

The worst part is going to be the "receptions"—a sort of endless cocktail party with strangers, lasting three months. I don't want to know any more strangers at my age, don't like parties, and have been on the water wagon for the last six weeks on purpose—to be in practice against American hospitality. I am not a teetotaler by nature, but I don't want to follow in the footsteps of Dylan Thomas or Brendan Behan in that continent.

How difficult it is going to be, to keep sober and polite with the same questions from everybody and hardly any life of one's own! Perhaps Carol will be able to shelter me a little and plead for time off in which to see Marineland and Disneyland and the Grand Canyon. The good part is seeing America, the bad part is being seen.

We spent the day trying to cut our luggage weight, so as not to have to pay hundreds of pounds in excess baggage by air. I can only afford to present two suits to my public, but we can take extra clothes for the *Queen Elizabeth* and leave them in New York. For a young lady like Carol this is very reasonably a sort of dress show and series of cocktail parties, but for me it is only the necessity to offer some sort of façade on the allowance of forty pounds air weight.

It is horrifying how little clothing you can take economically when you also have a camera and lecture slides and notebooks and even the weight of an electric razor.

In one way, you have to plot it like an expedition to the North Pole. Should we take Pemmican? Would sleigh dogs be economical if we ended by eating them? This is not quite as exaggerated as it sounds. If it is a question of one-night stands, it becomes a question of laundry. If it is a question of laundry, you must take drip-dry shirts and underclothing, because ordinary washing will never catch up with you. Most English drip-dry clothing is non-porous to sweat, with the result that the thinnest shirts are like wearing a Turkish bath. (The answer to this particular fraction of the problem seems to be to buy drip-dries when you get to America, where porous shirts are said to be available.) And will your suits get creased with all the packing? And how heavy are shoes!

My recollection of America during the fall and winter is that everybody is baking hot indoors and freezing cold outside. So you have to have light indoor clothing with a heavy topcoat. And how heavy, and how cumbersome (for instance in California) is my tweed ulster!

Apart from the two hundred pounds or so that we might have had to pay in overweight if we considered our vanity, there is the fact of carrying the luggage itself. Luggage is an excellent word. You lug it about. In America, porters are almost an extinct race, so you have to be ready to lug your own.

We have bought wheels which can be strapped to our valises.

We have proudly stuck first-class Cunard labels on everything.

19 · 9 · 63

There is something faintly horrible about the *Queen Elizabeth,* as if a super cinema (rather out of date) had broken off from Hyde Park Corner and sailed away to sea. She is very empty. You wander through the colossal lounges and Wurlitzer-type tea gardens, thinking of Fitzgerald and the Great Gatsby. She was built in 1939-40, presumably under the cultural influence of that period—you expect to meet gay, elderly flappers singing excerpts from *The Girl Friend*—but went straight into action as a troop ship. She was recommissioned in 1946, with what must have been the original décor as planned. Wilkinson, Eric Gill (?), megalythic murals. Everything is comfortable, serviceable, grandiose, dated—but where is the Great Gatsby? The vulgarity of Metro-Goldfish has caught up with her.

For a small-boat sailor like me, who has been bucketing round Alderney for seventeen years, there is something unseamanlike about this Hollywood colossus—are we 85,000 tons? Yet she has braved the high seas for twenty-three years with impunity, and the greatest dignity, as seen from outside. Meeting her off Alderney or Cherbourg in one of my two little *Popsies,* she presented a broadside of mighty grace. She once solemnly dipped her ensign to *Popsie I* (a 14-foot sailing dinghy) like Queen Victoria bowing to a miniature poodle. Nothing can make her look anything but wonderful in outline—beautiful lines—it is only the interior that is garish.

She has made two round trips a month for less than a generation, yet is already out of date and headed for the scrap heap eight years hence. What countless millions in gold, what activity and organization have been outmoded in this brief lifetime!

I don't object to her inside for being in a past mode. The inside of the *Cutty Sark,* the most beautiful ship on earth, is in a past mode.

It may be that colossal interiors become vulgarized? Yet I don't object to the interior of St. Peter's, Rome.

Perhaps I might object to St. Peter's if it were at sea, with a Palm Court orchestra?

I would like to feel sentimental about the *Elizabeth,* as I do about the *Cutty Sark,* but somehow I can't. Nobody on board that I have met this first calm, empty, gray afternoon seems to be fond and proud of her, as if she were a great lady. The officers look like businessmen in nautical dress doing slightly distasteful office work. Somehow a hotel ought not to be floating about on the "high seas."

The high seas, the high sierras, the haute école, the high and mighty, what have these got to do with the Stoll Picture House?

Dear Carol cried piteously on saying good-bye to her splendid parents at Waterloo, but the painful scene was cut short by time. Our drive from Walton-on-Thames was a breakneck business, agonized by traffic blocks, and we only caught the boat train by *two minutes.*

We passed fairly close to Alderney at ten to eleven P.M. this evening, watching the little lights from our great boat deck and wishing everybody well. For not the first time at night I was counting the five flashes of the Casquets and the four of Monez long before we were certain of them. How often, from small boats in wet seas, and sometimes through rain or fog, I have counted these same flashes as a matter of self-preservation.

In this Leviathan you have the deceptive feeling that if you ran into the Channel Islands you would sink them.

By the long time it took to reach Alderney from Cherbourg, I suppose the coastal tide must have been against us. I thought of my dear dog Jenny behind one of those lights with a pang.

20 · 9 · 63

We are accompanied by a few gannets in all stages of plumage that can fly. They must be starting their winter sojourn at sea. There is a little-used deck called the Gallery Deck, which you reach through an iron door, and from here you can watch our forefoot slicing ponderously up and down through the long, smooth Atlantic swell, and realize you are at sea. At least you can see the sea and feel the wind. "Indoors," which is the only word you can use for it, there is nothing to prove we are a ship except the creaking of the veneers, the gain and loss of your own body's gravity, the step of the staircase which rises to meet your foot, and the occasional crabwise courses across the polished floor.

It is a good idea to keep a porthole open, so that at least you do hear the sea.

Facts. The keel was laid in 1933. The then Queen christened her on September 27, 1938. As a troopship in the war she conveyed 811,324 persons and steamed 492,635 miles. Her overall length is 1,031 feet and if she were set on end she would be almost as high as the Chrysler skyscraper. As it is, the right way up, from keel to masthead she is about as high as Alderney (234 feet). Her gross tonnage is 83,673, her officers and crew 1,290, her passenger capacity 2,225. The letters of her name on the bows cover 60 feet. She is driven by oil-fueled turbines, her three whistles weigh a ton each, she has 10 million rivets, 2,000 portholes and 37 public rooms. My secret Gallery Deck seems hitherto unknown to man. There are several lifts (elevators), pantries, restaurants, etc., in which members of the crew have been lost and forgotten for many years, and there they subsist on spiders and old photographs of Greta Garbo.

This morning I was the only occupant of the swimming pool, this evening there were two others.

The waves inside the swimming pool mimic the waves outside it, in the sea. If you are going to dive, and weigh over sixteen stone as I do, it is advisable to notice which end of the pool the water has tilted to. The deep end tends to become the shallow end from one moment to another.

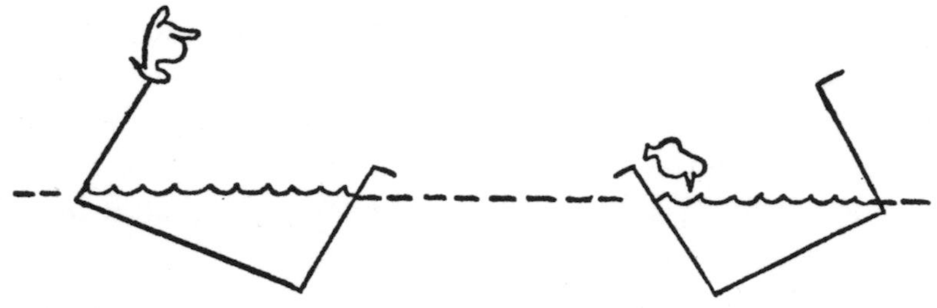

I made friends with the attendant, who was informative about buying a plastic cover for my own pool in Alderney. I tipped him five dollars and he promised to write for addresses to a friend of his who has an outdoor pool near Boston. The advantages of a plastic cover are a) that it would tend to retain heat at night (my heating bill is eight pounds a week), b) that it would help to discourage algae, which he believes to breed at night, and c) that at least it would keep out the tree leaves, pollen, seeds, etc., during the hours of darkness. I asked him to post his information to Harry Griffiths—who is meanwhile writing to Admiral of the Fleet Lord Ernle Erle Drax on the same subjects. I looked down on one of these plastic covers while I was flying over Guernsey a fortnight ago.

I asked the maître d'hôtel not to give us a table for two but to put us where there were young people who would be company for Carol. For the last two meals we have been at a table with a New Zealander who has a daughter of twenty and a Bostonian with a pleasant son of sixteen. We get on very well. The Bostonian's wife died 20 months ago and he has been touring Scandinavia and Germany, etc., with the son, whom he adores in his bereavement. He has invited us to a cocktail party in the Observation Lounge at 7:15, and we have dressed for dinner. This is the first time, after a lovely bathe in the salt pool and a hot shower of fresh water, that I have put on the new midnight blue dinner jacket which is to be part of the lecture act. I feel clean and younger and sad that I am on the water wagon.

Carol, whose going-away bouquets make our little passageway look like a flower shop, also got invited to a party by the Purser, but had to refuse because of the prior engagement. I wasn't. I pretended to be jealous.

After a cheerful dinner at which we had crêpes Suzette, I spent rather a sad evening in the Main Saloon, observing what the Natural Selection of human competition in practice has chosen to be the ideal human being. If these people were traveling First Class on the *Queen Elizabeth,* they had proved themselves to be what we consider First-Class People. They were Ideal Man.

The Ideal Human is nearly sixty years of age. It takes that long to succeed. His or her distorted body is expensively but not tastefully dressed. One point in favor is that the face definitely has character. It is on the whole an evil and greedy character, but it is strong. The expression is sharp, common and discontented, though the happier ones do have a sort of bloated bonhomie, like bookies. They do not look particularly ill-natured. When not gambling they tend to look bored. Their most striking characteristic is utter stupidity, underlaid by obstinacy and narrow-minded herd instinct. Some have cunning. A poker face is common, still in repose.

The depressing thing about them was their occupation. They were passing the time, not employing it. Their passtime was either to watch a film by Walt Disney or else, as in the case of my lot, to make small bets on wooden horses whose movement depends on the throw of dice. They ended their intellectual, upper-class divertimento with two games of Bingo.

The horses were moved on the green baize by an "able seaman" and the numbers were called with false jocularity by a junior officer. What were sailors doing, what were mariners doing, in evening dress, shoving those ignoble horses about and trying to be "the life and soul of the party" as they chirruped about "clickety-click" for sixty-six?

And what am I doing in this galley? Have I striven for 57 years so as to play Bingo with raddled old ladies in wigs? Is this success? Am I the Ideal Man?

Could any of these people read a book, and, if so, why were they playing Bingo instead of reading one?

I came away at about 11 P.M., when I could stand it no longer, and am off to bed (not bunk) to read a Penguin.

God save us all.

21 · 9 · 63

I have come to the conclusion that what I don't like about the *Elizabeth* is only her interior decoration. Nothing can save it now except extreme old age. If it could be preserved for 200 years, our descendants might be able to condescend, sympathize or even admire, but for the time being it is cheap beyond words. Strange to use the word "cheap" in connection with this fantastic outlay of specie, but it is the cheapness, the vulgarity, that has nothing to do with money.

At breakfast I asked the headwaiter about the enormous, hideous tapestry of Aphrodite which dominates the main dining hall. It is a terrible, distant reminiscence of Botticelli's Venus, and the waiter says it was designed and made by eight nuns working for (I think it was) six years. It is about six yards square. You can't help feeling a certain pity for it, when you think of those poor well-meaning nuns with their crippled ideas of sex and beauty, but oh what a waste of hopeful effort—how many billion useless threads.

The taste of the objects displayed in the shops on the main deck is something pitiful—pottery gnomes and bunnies and china tankards with monkey faces.

If I find this sort of thing in America I will try to sympathize and condone it, but it is inexcusable in a civilization (Anglo-Norman) that has lasted nearly a thousand years.

I found a first-rate remark in Richard G. Stern's *Golk* last night. "T.V. has the best of the movie traits, the camera directing the audience to any aspect of the scene, any detail, unusual or otherwise, which will best express the flow of the story, plus accentuating music, special visual effects, and so on. So you can hit harder, quicker, *and with fewer words* than you can on the stage." It applies also to movies. I must remember this tip when I write for the English TV.

We have a good breeze on the port beam which, with the speed of our own passage, makes it hard to open the iron door to the gallery deck and blows a grand spume to starboard above the bone in our teeth.

Cabled Colston Leigh saying, "Are you meeting us or what is our hotel T. K. White."

Played squash for half an hour with the pro, before bathing in the pool. It must be the first game of squash racquets I have had for thirty years. I began by vaguely waving the racquet at the ball, some six inches away from it (it is a slow and rather dark court) but ended by taking four games out of nine. Of course the young man was favoring my bad leg, but at least I could whang the ball a bit. In fact I placed it smartly between his shoulders three times, scoring shots which he got in the way of, and he certainly hopped. By the end, we were both surprised and pleased at my moderate efficiency. A pretty lady spectator accosted me, saying, "I think you are very brave." Afterwards a long, glorious float in the green, salty swimming pool—the only occupant. Hungry as a hunter.

The poor little library is in a state of chaos. It is run by a touching elderly officer who sadly confesses he "is new to the job." He has two indexes—which are of no use to him, because the books are on the shelves in no discernible order. There are two good bird books (sea birds) in the index; but I did not have the time to look through all the books on the shelves for them.

Carol went to the film with the New Zealand girl. I read, learned lecture notes and had a second swim. When I float on my back with my hands folded on my belly, I am slightly right wing down. Is this the weight of my liver? Are people asymmetrical in weight? Does the heart on the left balance the liver on the right?

At supper the band played *Camelot* and our table had a special roast to itself, also a special Baked Alaska Pudding. Afterwards I watched Homo Sapiens playing Bingo, and paid for two games for Carol. First-Class Man has lips that turn down at the corners. So far as I can see, he has discovered that life is bloody and that it wasn't worth while being first class. So he plays Bingo.

22 · 9 · 63

The first Cunarder, the *Britannia*, sailed in 1840. Her hull could have fitted into one of our funnels. The *Mayflower* sailed 343 years ago. She weighed as much as our rudder (140 tons). We flatter ourselves with these comparisons, but they are the wrong ones to make. Our real grandeur is that we are a speck, but a speck, on the vast, inimical, dangerous wastes which we traverse—that there is probably nothing within hundreds of miles of us—that we are a flea crossing Trafalgar Square—that an accident could plunge all 83,000 tons of us to the bottom of the ocean, uncharted, unnoticed, without one trace of a ripple on any shore.

Carol stayed up late last night, drinking and dancing with Philip Kelly, whom she likes. We are having the better side of the clock in this direction—an extra hour's sleep every night. Coming back, we shall have an hour less for dancing.

There are a few petrels, or shearwaters, but I am too ignorant to distinguish between them at a distance. Also there are a few white horses on today's sea. What a steady and beautiful boat this is, as a boat. What with her own lines and the stabilizers, our smooth roll of less than 10° takes about 35 seconds from one position to the same one.

I took seven games out of nine off the young squash pro this morning, but of course he was being gentle with me. He said, "You must come back tomorrow, it would be a shame to stop now." Old men like this sort of flattery. All it means is that if he places the ball for me to hit, seven times out of nine I can place it where he can't return it as gently. I was amazed to find I am not very stiff.

Our sirens are lower bass A and they are wonderful—the blow of the greatest whale in the world, the bellow of leviathan.

This afternoon Carol and the other children went off to the cinema, the usual Hollywood stuff, while I spent a miserable hour or two gazing at my wretched lectures. They are boring, ill-composed and I deserve to be hanged for them. They seem more and more meaningless.

We have run into a colder wind from Newfoundland or somewhere and the swimming pool seemed warmer.

23 · 9 · 63

Carol stayed up till 3 A.M. with her young friends, causing Mr. Kelly to get up from bed and go in search of Philip. They sang and enjoyed themselves, and there had been a perfectly frightful hat parade for fancy dress hats.

Today is the end of my happy holiday at sea, and already with packing and form-filling the ten-week crucifixion begins. I dread these forms and queues and tickets, between receptions.

I took the squash pro to eight-all twice. I have always been fairly good at knowing my place in life. As a writer I am fair second class, as a poet hopeless, as a squash player wearing glasses (which I have to leave off) and hopping on one claudicated leg at the age of fifty-seven I know how much the pro is simply knocking up for me. But I can't help feeling pleased that I can even see the ball and hit it after all these years. Swimming was splendid afterwards, and even Carol turned up.

I have left out all about the rot like ship's newspapers and quizzes and guessing the day's run (about 740 miles) and the other fatuous means of keeping us amused, like a children's tea party for old bores.

Today the captain flattered us on the ship's notice board by writing that the sea was rough, with a heavy swell. It did not prevent racquets or overflow the swimming pool.

I have been eating too much. When you pay about two hundred and forty pounds for a ticket, you try to get your money's worth out of sheer meanness. From the pool and the racquets court alone, I have had my money's worth. When we come back, the *Elizabeth* will be at overhaul and we shall have to use the *Queen Mary*. She has no squash court. The one she had has been converted, somebody told me, into a jukebox for the teen-agers! Well, such is progress.

24 · 9 · 63

Last night we had a nice little gale of force 8 or 9, which the beautiful ship rode through like the Queen she is. This morning we were early on deck to photograph the statue of Liberty and watch the great backdrop of Manhattan and see ourselves dock. Then the bore of immigration and customs—who were not so hard on us as we feared—and Mrs. Grant and Ed Watkins were in the reception hall to meet us. We made friends at once.

Lunch was with Colston Leigh at the Roosevelt, after which we spent hours at the office talking over the routes and business details.

Our hotel is the Roger Smith on Lexington Avenue at 47th Street. It is sumptuous. My double bedroom with bath is more than six yards square, all in gray, with six lamps, a sofa and four armchairs and a TV set. A good color print over the beds and a desk which I am writing at and a thick fitted carpet. Carol says it is not very expensive and that hers is a nice room too.

Colston Leigh is a person of strong character and opinions who has definite ideas about lecturing in America, which he put across in a skillful pep talk.

America, said he, *is not a nation.* It is lots of nations with no definite background of common culture. so it is looking for a culture. My audiences will from the start be biased in my favor, expecting me to be a respected and lovable emissary of culture who has come to help them to get some. (How gladly I will try to offer it.) They won't want me to produce a tedious and reassured set lecture—particularly not to read it to them—yet they will expect me to have put some preparation into my extempore talk. All I have to do, says Colston Leigh, is be myself and let them love me and be nice to them. This seems reasonable.

The beef at the Roosevelt was thick, tender and succulent. New York, as ever, is the wonder of the world. Since I was last here they have got far ahead with building a new bridge to Staten Island. It will have a larger span than the Golden Gate, but why all this fuss about being "larger"? It is inevitably gigantic, it is of a splendid brick red, and I loved it on sight, in the morning sun.

How this mighty city is still changing! After only three years there are whole new skyscrapers.

I am very glad to be back in America and will try to be worthy of it and of England.

Carol is working like a trooper and remembers her way about better than I do. Mrs. Grant is a pet and everybody at her office was helpful.

It did not take us long to discover that my favorite of all skyscrapers, hitherto viewed from a distance, is right in the next block to our hotel on Lexington Avenue. Carol from a map says it may be the Waldorf-Astoria.

We had a first-rate meal at the hotel in the evening for about $4.50. In fact, it was fresher and less deep frozen than on the *Elizabeth* and quite as much as we needed to eat. The Roger Smith hotels are exactly on our level, really good without being fabulously expensive.

Carol has been bleating all day because she says the pavements are still rocking as if we were aboard ship. I am a stern master to her and give no sympathy to these plaints. Colston Leigh cheered her up a good deal by pretending to be a suitor. He is sixty and married the daughter of a Mormon bishop, so he says.

Manhattan is a small city in the horizontal. It is only enormous vertically.

25 · 9 · 63

Up and out early this morning, to buy a plain razor at the nearest drugstore, because of the round plugs on my English electric one which won't fit the flat holes of America. No electrician in any part of the world has ever been able to standardize anything. Even in the same town in England you get every diversity of fitting. Even in the same house. Something ought to be done about electricians, by law. Electrocution perhaps. Also about builders and about compilers of indexes for gardening catalogues and cookery books. Believe it or not, I have a cookery book at home in which the pages are numbered inside, i.e. at the spine, not on the outer edge of the page.

Breakfast at the drugstore when Carol got up, about 8:20, and afterwards to the Colston Leigh office, where Mr. Leigh, in great humor, gave us another long lecture about lecturing. Till luncheon we were fixing business details about money, taxes, work permits, etc.

While there we met Sir Hugh Foote, who claimed that he always crossed the Atlantic by air, not boat, because he lived in the future and did not want to waste time on the present—or rather meaningless words to this effect. He was jolly and public-relationly and I wondered what part of the Empire he would be giving away next. He had been here on some business to do with the United Nations.

Ivan von Auw came to lunch with us at the hotel where we had a good meal and a gossip about literary business.

After lunch Carol went off to make contact with an ancient

friend called Kahn, widower of opera singer Frieda Hempel, who lives on the tenth floor.

I resorted to my own bedroom where I spent an utterly miserable two hours trying to learn my lectures. I have been so aged by the last four years that nothing will stick in my brain. Anyway, the lectures are complete bosh and it was heartbreaking to practice them in front of a mirror. There are dozens of difficult poems, like Hopkins on Despair, which simply won't stick in my head. It will be professional suicide as a lecturer to do all the reading that I am going to have to do.

At five I was summoned to tea on the tenth floor, which included dinner afterwards and went on till 8:30, when I am writing this, again alone at last and about to struggle with more memorizing.

The pet skyscraper is not the W. Astoria. It is the General Electric. Its crown is gilt, but not at present illuminated.

26 · 9 · 63

I spent a wretched morning trying to get these futile lectures into my head and to memorize great blocks of Georgian poetry. My poor old head, once a serviceable one, is full of cotton wool.

In the afternoon we took the Tryon bus on 5th Avenue and went all the way to the terminus at the Cloisters, where we spent half an hour and came back by the same route. It gives a wonderful slice through New York up to something like 180th Street and, although not being allowed to smoke in the bus nearly slew me, I did enjoy every minute of the sunny, hazy, fall afternoon.

What ornament, what naïve invention, there is in the youthful architecture of this magnificent city! It has every style from Rameses to Aubrey Beardsley—the latter, a sort of fantasia of the year 1900—flourishing on the higher West Side.

It is fashionable to say that New York is dirty. I don't find it so. It has been fashionable to condescend to American business and city architecture, saying that it is hotchpotch, etc. I find it stimulating and packed with interest. One large building which we flashed past, made about the turn of the century, had enormous brownstone grotesque statuary in relief round its upper story—a truly hideous preview of Walt Disney's dwarfs—which was so ghastly, so massive and so startling that it compelled attention, even admiration. For at least the last fifty years these people have been trying to establish a style of their own, borrowed from Europe but transmuted here. Quite apart from the skyscraper mode, which is wholly their own and Sierra's, there is a distinctive American "classicism," which includes Corinthian columns of novel proportions, a sort of Aubrey Beardsley acanthus, and eagles in various attitudes. Why shouldn't it? Why shouldn't you combine Gothic with Doric for that matter, if you feel that way?

Incidentally, there is the other direction in which a skyscraper can ornament itself, besides its top, and that is by having flagstaffs with clean, huge flags protruding from the piano nobile. It makes the broad streets gay and fluttering.

We had glimpses of Harlem and the Bronx and the culture of *West Side Story*, but things were not slummy or gloomy or at all dangerous-looking in the autumn sunshine, and we passed through zones of skin color from Caucasian to Negroid without feeling that anybody was menacing or poor. I could see no slums like Glasgow's, or London's for that matter. The Negroes moved with a loping grace and I saw one particularly beautiful youth of about nineteen, a pensive coffee-colored Hamlet in splendid physical trim. The patrons of our bus were friendly and fairly well dressed. We were not actually in Harlem or Bronx.

Some of the exhibits at the Cloisters, at least two among many undoubted treasures, struck me as being first-rate forgeries. When you have lived in Florence, you know with what genius and industry an Italian master-craftsman can forge.

In the evening we went window-shopping in Times Square and dined at a drugstore there. It is a place which does have a smell of danger.

Then home early to bathe and bed and struggle with the Georgians.

A fine day. New York is in the same latitude as Naples.

Incidentally, talking of electricians, I tried to hire a tape recorder today, to play my 8-inch, half-track spools at 7½ inches per second. After much trouble we located and took delivery of an alleged English model—which turned out to be playing both tracks at once! Gave up.

Do Tryon buses smell of curry powder, or do the people in them, or does the West Side of New York?

27 · 9 · 63

Carol said at breakfast, "You know, I don't think Americans are so speedy as they are supposed to be." "How so?" "Well, even in a good hotel like this one it takes two days to get the laundry back, like in London, and I can get Kodachrome films developed in Walton-on-Thames quicker than I can in 45th Street. Also they cost more to develop here." "I suppose they invented the idea of speedy service, and we have caught up with them." "I suppose so."

Labor seems to be the most expensive thing in America. Everything, including the home, is well equipped and understaffed. The railway stations lack porters, the hotels lack servants, and the porters and the servants are overpaid in consequence.

One of the things that impress Carol most is that we get clean sheets and towels every day, but you have to put against this that you never know when the maids will do your room and that when my air conditioner breaks down it takes several hours and telephone appeals to get anything done about it. If you do.

America is a bit like ancient Rome. She has her senators and presidents from families of power and riches. Roosevelts and Kennedys might just as well be Claudians or Acilians. We are their cultured Greeks, they our powerful Romans. So why not introduce slavery too? It worked very well under Hadrian, whose laws for slaves were enlightened. Why not solve the labor shortage by importing Costa Ricans, etc., without hindrance and using them to solve the problem of porters and room service? Why not employ people in menial capacities when they are not capable of higher employment? Surely people find their own level? Is it not better for a "poor" person, whether poor-white or poor-black, to be well employed as a slave in New York instead of being blown up in Birmingham, Alabama? People have been much too emotional about slavery since the early nineteenth century. It stands to reason that a slave is a valuable asset, just as much as a cow is to a farmer, and I have yet to meet the farmer who is stupid enough to maltreat his cows.

I don't mean that Negroes and Puerto Ricans should be slaves more than anybody else of another color. Any color should be suitable for slavery, so long as the slave is suitable as a slave.

I foresee a time when the President of the United States will be as powerful and vicious as Caligula. We are in Republican Rome at present, the Emperors of America have yet to seize power.

I can think of two things which the English do better than the Americans. They can grow grass, indeed they grow this better than anybody in the world, and they can develop Kodachrome properly. My transparencies (on English film) which came back today from a big Kodak shop near the Roosevelt Hotel are pitiful. Practically all trace of the rich color we get in England has been reduced to a sort of sepia wash.

Our first step will have to be an Augustus. Kennedy, a venerable statesman who has completed his seventh term of office and preserved the nation from the atomic bomb, will reluctantly accept the title of Father of His Country. Intrigue, regicide and absolute power will set in. It won't be far after that to reach Nero Capone, say a hundred and fifty years from now.

Today is the beginning of Yom Kippur, however it spells itself, so two-thirds of the taxi drivers of New York—a profession which is largely Jewish—went off the streets at six o'clock.

This evening Herb and Rita Gardner came to dinner and made us laugh. He is the cartoonist and author of *A Thousand Clowns*. I have caught a hideous cold to start my tour with, and can't write more about this charming couple till tomorrow, when they take us to Greenwich Village.

28 · 9 · 63

The Day of Atonement. There are so many Jews in New York that they have stopped thinking of themselves as a persecuted minority. This makes it easier to be friends with them, without condescension and self-pity and all that, just as equals. New York must be one of the best cities in the world to be a Jew in. Probably they condescend to goys in Israel, just as we condescend to them in England, but here the relationship is easy.

In the morning we went to the wonderful Metropolitan Museum where I fell in love with the armor and also with the fountains and statues by Carl Milles in the restaurant.

They represent the five arts dashing away with inspirations from the spring of Aganippe on Mount Helicon. The periodic variation of the fountains is a legitimate device and, after some doubts, I accepted the airy, inhuman vivacity of the statues themselves. They are in a hasty gust of inspiration. Such a pity that the postcards of this fierce masterpiece are inadequate. I also bought myself a pair of cuff links made from tetradrachmae (Athenian fourpenny bits—four days' wages in silver) with the owl of Athena on them. We posted my old Fifth Avenue ones to Vito in Naples.

Everything in the Museum is wonderfully displayed. The greater riches of our London museums, and for that matter those also of Florence, Rome or Naples, are too crowded to stand comparison.

We lunched at the hotel—or rather, I did. Carol went off with old Mr. Kahn and ate her first oyster. I spent the afternoon till 5 o'clock struggling to memorize poetry.

Then Lou Wilson and Herb and Rita Gardner took us out for the evening. First we went on a tour of Greenwich Village and ate at rather an expensive restaurant called Pete's Back Yard.

The variegated and homely and astonishingly late-Victorian architecture of the Village will one day be recognized as strange and beautiful, just as John Betjeman has brought us to recognize Victorian Gothic. There is in particular a fantastic disused church of red brick which looks as if Doré had miscegenated with a brownstone baptistry and a lighthouse —that wild delirium of *fin de siècle* ecclesiasticism which seems to bear no relation to anything, or every relation to everything. It is abandoned and will no doubt be pulled down while this kind of taste is still in disgrace, but it will be a terrible pity to destroy it. It is strange that Gothic architecture has twice become funny—once under the influence of Harry Walpole and once under the asylum-waterworks style of encaustic tiles, etc.

Greenwich Village architecture is so varied and astonishing that it can't fail to please, and its ugliest extravaganzas have a *succès de scandale.*

The whole ramshackle little milieu (why all these French words—is it something to do with the Bohemianism of the place?) is as it were homely provincial, a bit rowdy, but pleasant and not sinister in its violence.

Far the best thing we watched there was a game of basketball in the open air, played by beautiful young Negroes with happy faces, who sprang about inside their wire cage like panthers romping, or like the inspired Arts of the Metropolitan Museum. As physical specimens, the Aryans playing handball nearby were much inferior to these lithe, bounding, telescoping, deceptive bronzes. I was glad to see a couple of white boys on the two teams.

After dinner we went by taxi to Coney Island, whose season is now more or less over, and ate hot dogs and iced custards and nuts and popcorn and bubble gum. Lou distinguished himself as a marksman, shooting at moving tin ducks, and the lights and the sights and the youth and the gaiety were very like Blackpool.

There was one piece of complicated feeling—a large pet shop where, on paying an admission fee, you were allowed to go in and feed the animals. On the plus side of this exhibit, there was the fact that lots of people were paying to give love and presents to other mammals. This was good, and a rather pathetic plus mark for the compassion of Homo Sapiens. But oh, the thin puppies with worms, the pathos of animals in cages, the creatures unsuitable to such durance! There were even two red setters like Jenny, but skeletons, and a lovely Bonzoi fading away like a great actress with consumption, and a Saint Bernard whose brown eyes looked at me, saying, "Why this?" Besides, what happens to all those tottering puppies when they have lost the charm of puppyhood? After all, it is a business venture.

I talked to a raven and an owl and what I supposed to be a coon, but had to go apart from the others of our party with tears in my eyes. I wanted to buy them all and give them their liberty, but what would have been the result of that?

My leg became unserviceable by about 11 P.M. We went to the Gardners' apartment till about 1:15—very amusing, intelligent and friendly people who had kept fairly loyally to their Day of Atonement—then home to bed.

That St. Bernard. Life is an insoluble pain.

29 · 9 · 63

It poured rain all day, so we were cheated of our trip by boat round the island of Manhattan. Everybody says that this is a "must." Never mind, we will do it on some other visit. I have seen more of New York by bus and taxi and on foot in these few days than I did in three months from Julie's apartment in Cadillacs. The only intelligent trip I seem to have made then was on the Staten Island ferry, also with Lou. I find it a great help that I genuinely like and admire Americans, actors and children. All three are innocent and want to be loved. Nothing can alter the fact that New York is the greatest wonder of the world, and they have made it. Are making it. Skyscrapers still grow almost overnight. We might be living in Florence in the Renaissance.

Last night at Coney Island I drank root beer for the first time. It is like Coca-Cola. Most of the time we try to eat American food rather than English ones. Today it was swordfish for lunch—which is like a cross between salmon and mackerel or tuna—and I have had sturgeon (like sweet slices of India rubber) and bluefish, a bit like mackerel, and countless other novelties like pecan pie and blueberry pie and Yankee Pot Roast and waffles with maple syrup for breakfast, or, for the same meal, corned beef hash (like fish cakes made of corned beef). We have forgotten the names of half these novelties.

While I was talking with Herb it seems that Carol had a conversation last night with Rita and Lou about President Kennedy. She gave me a rather garbled account of it at lunch, saying that there are many rumors about Kennedy which will never become public because of his influence and wealth. There was something about his having been married before, wrong for Catholics, and something about quantities of women at the White House. Carol was maddeningly vague about what she had been told.

All morning and most of the afternoon, while Carol washed her hair and the rain rained, I plodded on trying to learn these grisly poems. It is enough to set you against poetry for life, and the thought of the lectures, so near now, scares me stiff.

30 · 9 · 63

For some reason I started a horrible stomachache at dinner last night, such as I have not had before. The stomach tight and swollen and pain even in the small of the back so that it was impossible to lie down. I was awake till about 4 A.M. trying to vomit or excrete or both and wishing the drugstores were open or that Room Service was obliging or that I had some plain English medicines like Veganin and Dr. Collis Browne's Chlorodyne. Am I starting a gastric ulcer or was it something I ate?

The vaunted "efficiency" of Americans, as Carol remarked, is partly a myth—perhaps due to labor shortage. The dining room staff here is most friendly and obliging, so are the bedroom maids. But the desk is standoffish and inhospitable, and the Negro who does the room service is surly and bullying—an elderly man perhaps brooding about the present events in Birmingham. The general setup is luxurious and reasonable as to price. Like everything in life, it is not all good—for people with stomachache. Some things even at Colston Leigh's, who is the best lecture agent in America, are less efficient than all that experience might have made them. I don't think he understands my income tax position and he quite forgot my labor permit. Outside my window they are building a new skyscraper and, as in England, the laborers seem to spend most of the time having coffee. Perhaps I am only grizzling because of my belly. One thing which is no myth is the general benevolence and drive toward goodness of Americans. The average American unfortunately shares with the average Englishman an infantile and rather bogus mystique for ball games. I spent much of yesterday watching baseball and football on TV. It was as fatuous and degrading as soccer in England, perhaps more so. The general pictographic level in America, the camera level, is lower than in England. Our TV and our photographic processes are above theirs.

Today begins the horror of packing again, and my lectures are only half learned.

Lunch at the Chateau Richelieu with Mr. Mong of the *Sat. Ev. Post,* a pleasant and intelligent young man. We discussed several ideas for fiction and illustrated articles (including Hadrian, and this tour). I asked him about the rumors Carol unearthed about President Kennedy and he said they were everywhere. In fact, he said, when Kennedy became the President Elect he was known jokingly as the President Erect.

We ought to find out whether our path will cross the paths of the touring companies of *Camelot* or of Herb Gardner's *A Thousand Clowns.* Also I have discovered the address of Marguerite Yourcenar (Northeast Harbor, Maine) and if she is not too far away from Boston for local transport, and if she would receive me, it would be pleasant to pay her my homage. I have written to tell her so, but probably the notice is too short. She may not get the letter while we are near Boston, and even that is far enough away from Northeast Harbor. She is said to be a recluse like Salinger, the only other American author I have ever written to.

More trouble today trying to buy flashbulbs which would fit my English holder. Also bought an adapter for my English razor (to American plugs) but that wouldn't fit either. The English end was too narrow! Really, some universal penal law ought to be passed against everybody everywhere who has anything to do with electricity. I have been reading a horrifying book called *One Hundred Years of Lynching,* which describes the terrible, slow and obscene deaths (slow roasting alive after emasculation, etc.) sometimes meted out to Negroes. Not elaborate enough for electricians. Perhaps we could electrocute them *on machines that didn't work.*

Many Negroes in New York have happy and beautiful faces. I saw one young, strong, clean male today with eyelashes which would have turned Elizabeth Taylor green with envy. Their thickness curved upward almost in a semicircle.

Carol observed at dinner tonight: "You know, the Americans eat much more than we do, yet they don't get any fatter." Her second discovery was: "The Americans give away more things free than we do. For instance, free matches, free side dishes and coffee at this hotel, free programs in the theatres, free timetables and all that." I shall keep a list of Carol's aphorisms.

Watched some All-In Wrestling on TV. It strikes me as being a little more convincing than All-In Wrestling in England, since it is a little less preposterously acrobatic. On the whole, TV in America is not up to the English standard—like grass and color printing. I see I am repeating myself, so I will go to bed.

Today my other leg went wrong and the ankle has swollen up like a pumpkin. I am on my feet all day.

Yesterday I saw some jade earrings in a shopwindow and remarked to Carol, "What a pity they are not cuff links, they are just my cup of tea." Today, when I came back from the Richelieu, there was a little present for me. A little one! Carol is the most wonderful person I know for giving *big* presents which have been thought out in secret. The little present was, of course, those identical jade earrings, reset as cuff links. I honestly jumped for joy and put them on at once, instead of the tetradrachmae.

I watched some more wrestling after going to bed. It is quite as preposterous as in England.

Some Negroes have square bottoms, like the statue of the late Roman emperor in the hall of the Metropolitan—or quadrilateral anyway.

I suppose I mean not round. Very muscular.

This is not a good drawing.

And some of their long, thin forearms, like spider monkeys, very graceful, and elegant fingers. They can walk with a beautiful lope.

1 · 10 · 63

The automat restaurant in the train to Albany—its most amazing device was a machine which gave change for paper money. In went a dollar bill which was inspected and out come four silver quarters. Why couldn't we put in bits of newspaper cut to the right size?

Our sunny train trip to Albany was mostly along the Hudson River, whose spacious woods and waters helped to confirm my suspicion that America is practically uninhabited and can never go to war with Russia or China, which are mostly uninhabited too. Wars are about territory, and the three nations have lots already.

Norman Rockwell is the right though now unfashionable artist for this sharp-edged, four-square, autumn-leafed, open-air paradise of sumac and poplar and silver birch and maple and acacia. Is the distribution of trees more worldwide than animals?

On a lake—which lake?—a great eerie graveyard of gray cargo ships, like an elephants' cemetery.

The gold of the trees runs from a greenish nine carat of the poplars to the deep red nugget of the sumacs. You see fewer birds from the train than you do in England. At one point on the journey we passed a superb example of American Gothic—Sherman's Island Arsenal. This ought to be photographed and investigated.

The undergraduate who met us had been to the Washington march for the Negroes and was the American counterpart of our English Ban-the-Bomb marchers—a good, intelligent boy who instantly fell in love with Carol. He observed, *re* the Negroes, that America is at present engaged on two cold wars.

Williamstown College is nothing short of superb. It made me want to be an undergraduate again. It is a sort of Colonial-architected Athens set down in the glory of these flaming forests without a visible building out of character. To that extent it is artificial. But all art is artificial. That is what the word means. It is an artifact.

Everybody was charming to me, and the audience at the lecture was sweetly on my side from the start, wanting me to win through and laughing at the poorest jokes. They asked intelligent questions afterwards and we teased each other and they clapped most generously for quite a time.

People's kindness can be overwhelming.

At 12:30, after private entertainment by and of the faculty, and after a tour of their wonderful theatre, I go to bed.

Remember the Smiths—but what was the initial? (W. J. Smith and wife Barbara Howes.)

We arrived at the beautiful old hotel at 5:15, went to faculty party at 5:45, ate a banquet, lectured at 8. I have been on the go all day, and tired and happy and in love with youth and beauty and idealism and this kind northern Greece.

We should write to people like this (Professor Connolly?) to thank them.

I did get one real laugh, when I asked what would happen if Queen Elizabeth fell in love with Richard Burton.

2 · 10 · 63

Spent the morning photographing some of the vernal though autumnal beauties of this place. The boys call it the Happy Valley, rather shyly, and though it may sound corny it is a good description. People who live in beautiful places tend to become good and happy. Carol and I both decided to come back. Perhaps we can fit in a short visit at the end of the trip.

Two nice boys drove us chattily all the way to the Albany airport, where we caught a turbojet for Boston. It was a sunny hazy morning with deep French ultramarine lakes in the rusty woodscape fifteen thousand feet below the sunlit Indian red of our ailerons, and the gray humps of the Berkshires stuck out of the haze like whales or elephants.

For breakfast I had eaten sausage pattie and blueberry muffin and seen, outside, the American version of the blue jay. On the way to the airport we saw a peculiarity of this country—a sort of tiny fairground where you could go and bounce on trampolines. We also noted with some dislike the architecture of Troy which, although it is a derivative of the Victorian American style, is gloomy and surly and not as funny as Charles Addams.

We came in to Boston by that rather frightening approach over the sea which I have made before—soon after an aircraft was shattered by gulls there. Father Sweeney and a pleasant undergraduate met us and kindly took us to see the *Constitution* ("Old Ironsides"). Both Carol and I are lovers of the *Cutty Sark,* so we specially asked for this when they offered to show us things. Also I wanted photographs of her to show to Harry.

Her keel was laid in 1794. In 1812 she fought the *Guerriere* and the *Java,* in 1815 encountered *Cyane* and *Levant.* By 1850 she was a school ship at Annapolis. She actually cruised to Atlantic, Gulf and Pacific ports from 1931 to 1934 and is still "in service but not commissioned"! I noticed her topmasts had been unshipped. She is said to have done 12½ knots under topgallant sails. She flew a flag of 15 stripes and 15 stars (we now have 50). Her most famous captain was Stephen Decatur, whom Nelson admired.

The *Guerriere* was a British frigate of 38 guns. She was dismasted and struck her flag to the *Constitution,* which was of 44 guns. The *Java* was also of 38 guns and suffered the same fate. *Cyane* and *Levant* were of about 25 guns each and were captured in a single action.

Old Ironsides was provisioned for a crew of 475. She is stout and serviceable.

It is funny, but with all my affection for America I find it difficult to write fairly about American ships beating English ones.

At 6:45 I had had a shower and changed to a dark suit when Fr. Sweeney came to take us out to dinner at the Algonquin Club. We met Fr. Shea, who is to introduce me tomorrow, and a professor from Harvard and his wife. The two fathers and Carol and I went off after dinner and had a wonderful taxi tour of Boston, Fr. Sweeney giving a running commentary on everything from Bunker's Hill to the Old State House.

We were impressed by the M.I.T. buildings, particularly the auditorium. Modern America is brilliant at Theatres. The chapel there did not succeed with me.

We ended up walking round Harvard, where again I felt the happiness of youth and learning, like at Williams College.

We got back joky and tired at about 11 P.M.

Both priests were merry and friendly and unshockable and very different from the clergy who used to be the tyrants of Ireland in my day.

The architecture of Boston does not interest me much. The early stuff is just the same as so much of England and the later fantasies are restrained—do not have the crazy abandoned charm of true American Gothic. As usual with practically all Graeco-Roman buildings in the American Classical style, the columns are too long for their capitals, or the capitals too broad for their pillars. *This is not a vice.* It is simply that the American version of the column happens to be like that. They do not observe the proportions of Greece or Rome, and, if they don't want to—well, please yourselves, say I.

One Ionic or Doric version had capitals which made it look like a thin man with big ears.

Carol is enjoying all the sightseeing and meeting new people and we both felt warmly for Fr. Sweeney, his justice and kindness and warmth and simplicity and hospitality. When I told them I had been prepared for baptism into the Catholic Church but had desisted at the last moment on discovering that I didn't believe a word of it, they both roared with unaffected laughter. I am afraid the taxi cost the Society of Jesus about $10.

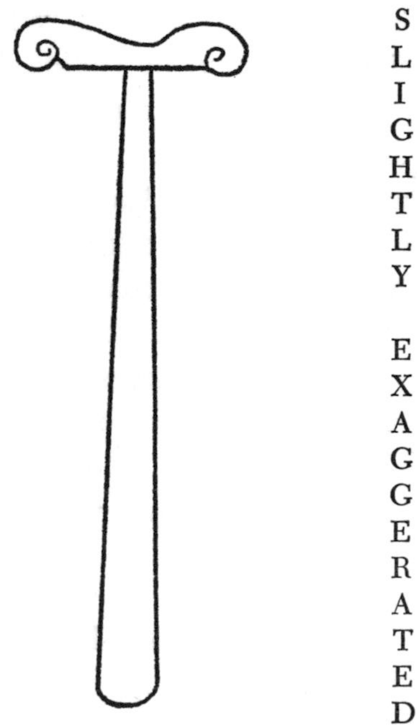

3 · 10 · 63

American architecture.

When a style is *recognizable* it becomes interesting.

All American architecture, both American Classical and American Gothic, is individual and recognizable and different from its originals. This is a good thing. I don't *want* the Caroline English architecture of Boston's Old State House. I suspect that I am not going to care for the correct imitation Gothic (circa 1920) of Boston College, where I lecture tonight. Imitation architecture is dead. I do sincerely enjoy

American Colonial—the stuff we had at Williams College—and the wilder flights of American Gothic, like that insane church in Greenwich Village. These, plus the skyscrapers, are the true vintage of America.

When I say this sort of thing to Americans who are hoping I will admire the Old State House for being English, I get afraid that they will think I am condescending. I am not. I honestly enjoy the true American style—there is no reason why you shouldn't be fond of what is funny, touching, *trying*. Their architecture *tries*. It is young and good and comical and individual and not jaded, and it is high time that these great people accept themselves without apology.

We shopped round Boston and photographed a few features. The three things which appealed to me were a) a nesting box for birds (in the park) in the shape of a Bavarian Castle! I longed to believe that any birds who had ever thought of nesting in it wore leather breeches and were known as *von und zu* by their respectful comrades. b) The bridge near the bird schloss is an inventive arrangement of white globes, as if Sherlock Holmes had mated with some small suspension bridges. c) There is a sort of large, striped ice-cream cone out of which there emerge the flames of a real flambeau. It stands at an intersection and has something to do with the Community Chest, so a taxi driver told us.

After luncheon at a Chinese restaurant we drove out to photograph Boston College, at Chestnut Hill, where I am to lecture tonight. It is beautifully done, with all the restraint of the best late Victorian or Edwardian or indeed Georgian colleges at Oxford (England) and is a feat of serious Gothic imitation. But why be slaves? Why imitate Lincoln Cathedral, or any other cathedral, so faithfully? These things have been *done,* and what we want of the Americans is that they should invent, not copy or continue too academically. Why sham that you are living in the Middle Ages? If you must be Gothic, develop it somehow or other. Chestnut Hill is beautiful and idealistic, but it is in a dead mode.

The taxi driver had never heard the famous rhyme about Boston, that it is

> The land of the bean and the cod
> Where the Lowells talk to the Cabots.
> And the Cabots talk only to God.

It is a rhyme which does throw light on some of my lack of sympathy for this city. It is too conservative, too snobbish, tries too successfully to be in "ghastly good taste." One foot of Boston is still, almost regretfully, in Charles the First's Lincolnshire.

Our hotel there is a vast megalopolis for flappers of the 1920's, now very old and doddery. It has among its countless company rooms an oval ballroom, calculated for debutantes of that day, in which you faintly seem to hear the strains of "Who Stole My Heart Away?" Yet it has more individuality than Boston College, was once built in a then living idiom, and has remained true to *Chu Chin Chow* and *The Girl Friend* and Ivor Novello. We are among the very few guests tended by its inadequate staff, but it seems able to subsist on conventions and birthday parties.

4 · 10 · 63

I will always remember last night's lecture happily. It was the first time in my life I have had what they call a "standing ovation"—one of the audience said afterwards that I recited like Richard Burton—and another one told Carol, not me, that it was the best lecture he had ever had. Anyway, I feel I am getting to understand the job.

Afterwards we had a reception for about thirty undergraduates, nice boys as usual, who went on talking till past eleven o'clock. A healthy thing was that these Catholic students could and did express dissatisfaction with the Jesuitical teaching of philosophy and ethics, in front of their pastor and master, Fr. Sweeney. The gist of their complaint was that reading in philosophy was censured—that only Catholic authors were furnished to them and they could not even discover the names of anti-Catholics. Everything, they said, was referred to St. Thomas Aquinas, and everything not reconcilable to him was simply omitted. I did not want to make an issue of the matter by encouraging too much rebellion. As Fr. Sweeney's guest, I was not there to subvert his doctrines. So I made a joke of the complaint (a complaint made seriously—they were practically appealing to me to furnish them with the names of non-Catholic philosophers) and suggested that if they were as persecuted as they claimed to be, they had better go underground and make a resistance movement. They replied that if they did, they would be disciplined by being sent to summer school.

I was pleased that these boys should be allowed to be "agin

the government," while still being furnished with a discipline which our English beatniks have lacked, and our long, pleasant, intelligent conversation covered everything from Ban-the-Bomb to the purchase of marijuana—which they promised to arrange for me. A bright, cultured, well-meaning, not dead-minded, slice of American youth—just as keen, but not as mannered or jaded, as the English undergraduate who nowadays competes drearily at the University for a degree which will qualify him for a job on the Establishment.

All were warmhearted and alive, and as grateful to me as I was to them.

How much more wonderful than the "receptions" I had dreaded!

This morning we were away early, after trouble at the airport about canceled flights, in rather a tatty Constellation of Eastern Airways. It is the aircraft with three rudders. Her four engines carried us the 193 miles to New York in about an hour, at 10,000 feet, Long Island Sound gleaming silver on our port wing, through coveys of flocking cloudlets.

Carol is settling down to our routine as to the manner born, and holds a court or circle of her own at the reception.

After luncheon we had a long business conference at Colston Leigh's, and then took the Fort Tryon bus, to rediscover the building with the grotesques on it and photograph them. We reached it eventually at the intersection of Ft. Washington Avenue and 181st Street. It was a disappointment. Instead of being interesting and individual, as it had seemed when we whisked past it in the bus, it was in fact actively horrible—perhaps the most hideous building in the world.

There are three of them in a row, apartment houses, and whoever designed these enormous dwarfs must have been an evil Teuton on the verge of insanity.

I have been insular and ill-informed on the subject of American architecture. I keep thinking in terms of the English styles of Classical or Gothic. But New York is a polynational Metropolis, and there is no reason why its art should not derive from Florence or the châteaux of the Loire, or, for that matter, from Assyria, Egypt and Babylon. In fact, this is exactly what it often does do. There is no reason why the stone face of a New York mansion should not be ornamented with incised letterings in Hebrew or Yiddish, and sometimes they are. I must remember that the basis of American art is cosmopolitan.

It would be a good idea to take a survey of the radiators of automobiles, from the architectural point of view. They have an Assyrian (?) feeling, a touch of Moloch or Baal.

Remember that young barefooted beatnik sitting in the famous chapel of M.I.T., listening to his friend playing Bach on the organ above his head. He was rapt, his lean, starved, dirty hands folded passively, and at first I thought he was a down-and-out religious maniac practicing yoga.

Americans are fond of putting spikes on odd parts of their buildings, presumably to deter the birds. For instance, they sometimes put a sort of fringe, like eyebrows or eyelashes, above the lintels of windows. Also they can put sawlike metal strips on porches, to prevent loiterers' sitting down.

Here is an oddity to add to the change machine in the train's automat, which could give change for dollar bills.

In Long Island, fishermen can buy live *worms* from slot machines!

5 · 10 · 63

We started off at 11:30 in the Circle Line river boat from Pier 83 (advertised, but 81 in fact) for the famous 3-hour tourist trip round Manhattan Island. It is said to be 35 miles and take three hours. We blew off dozens of photographs. (I accounted for 60 myself.)

Only two facts have stuck in my head.

First, the best bridges are those with two layers of traffic. (It doubled the expense of the bridge, so somebody told me three years ago.) But, if so, why not three layers? How would a bridge look with half a dozen layers, or more? What are the engineering problems involved?

The Queensborough still remains my favorite of all bridges, because of the crown- or artichoke-like objects with which it decorates its prodigious piers. I believe it was made in 1900. Other bridges may be more graceful, but none so massively eccentric.

The other fact I noticed is that Manhattan really consists of two clusters of skyscrapers—the cluster at Wall Street end and the Midtown cluster. I don't think it will be many years until these two fill up the gap between them.

My trouble with a camera is that when I like an object I want a four-square photograph of it, not a "clever" one such as the modern artist might prefer. The only modernistic pictures I may have taken (with the telescopic lens) were of a heap of used automobiles, a real Chinese junk with a speedboat passing it, and a skyline of water towers.

To a stranger the four most unusual things about New York are 1) the steam coming out of holes in the road, 2) the fire escapes, 3) the air conditioners in so many windows, and 4) the skyline of water storage tanks.

I tried for pictures of all these. In the afternoon, as Carol wanted to write letters home, I went off to Greenwich Village by myself to photograph the Doré church and other individual features. One is called the Jefferson Market Courthouse. Greenwich Village has more of what I call American architecture than anywhere else.

American architecture is based on severely straight lines, with fantastic decoration between. Originally functional, traditional and vernacular, it was invaded by ornament in the middle of the nineteenth century.

Last night I bought an excellent paperback called *Made in America* by John A. Kouwenhoven. I have not had time to read it, and won't have for many weeks, but there are several interesting points in its illustrations. 1) In 1876, the Americans were *decorating* their machinery. You could have a Corinthian pillar in your steam engine. 2) Prefabricated houses were obtainable in the same year (Barnard's Portable Patent Houses were exhibited and sold in St. Louis, Missouri, in 1847), and in 1890 you could buy a *stamped metal house-front*. The Grover and Baker Sewing Machine Company had a frontage at 495 Broadway of *Gothic cast iron and glass*. The illustration shows it to have been splendidly elaborate. How Beckford would have loved to have had one at Fonthill! (Or probably not. It is quite as mad as Fonthill, but in a different mode of madness.)

Dinner this evening at the Château Richelieu cost me forty dollars for myself, Carol, Lou Wilson and tip. Afterwards Lou took us to a sort of cabaret with a minimum cover charge of six dollars each. It was at a place called Upstairs at the Downstairs, or something like that. The entertainment was well-meaning, laborious, wishy-washy and mildly pleasant—not mean, like *Beyond the Fringe*. Then we had coffee at an expensive coffee house opposite and got home at midnight.

I indulge in these frolics for Carol's sake. My own old bones would rather be home in bed—particularly as we have a brunch party tomorrow at 11:30, by which time we must be packed and ready for our next passage—to North Carolina.

I noticed at the cabaret that some American males may perhaps tend to have more protrusive funny bones than those of other nations. Two of the actors and one in the audience had elbows a little like the ones which are emphasized in Popeye and other American cartoons. It may be a real biological variety. White American males also tend to have huge and shapeless buttocks.

6 · 10 · 63

Yesterday my cabdriver was teasing me. He drew up beside a van at an intersection and pleaded with the van driver to let us pass, explaining that I was going to have a baby. The van man replied in a beautiful Brooklyn accent, "So what does he have a baby for? Six you gotta have now." It was in reference to the recent birth of quintuplets.

This morning, part of a procession crossed our Avenue. It was led by an Irish band, dressed in the gay imaginary kilts and plaids which the sentimental New Yorker fondly believes to exist in the Emerald Isle. They looked like Scottish soldiers dipped in green ink.

On Friday I bought a book of Beatnik poetry by the poets of Greenwich Village. It is called *The Beat Scene,* illustrated with excellent photographs of them, and a horrid fate is befalling me. I am beginning to understand and sympathize with the Beatnik! Their philosophy is old-fashioned—Nihilism. You reject everything that has led to the atomic bomb—i.e., that has led to now. So you reject manners, shaving, washing, clean clothes, money, rhyme, meter, morals, in fact the whole civilization that has produced the present. It is an interesting and partly valid experiment. The trouble is that if you reject everything, you must also reject writing at all and, if carried to a logical conclusion, you must reject being alive.

The Beatniks of this book are pathetically sincere, almost sentimental, but not notably intelligent. The fact is that if you live in a gregarious society, you must accept a few social rules as a *modus vivendi.* They demand that I should put up with their verminous beards, which I gladly do, but they ought in return to make some sort of concession to my modes of deportment. I am myself an agnostic and an anarchist. I have no objection to their drugs or homosexuality or promiscuity or free verse or not washing. Only, if they won't wash, they don't attract me socially. I have a right to reject the Beatniks for smelling and not working as hard as I do, just as they have a right to reject me.

I don't reject them. There is something young and touching and hopeful hidden under their grubby effort. It is misdirected—but they are youthful, and will get directed by the facts of life all too soon.

I asked Lou Wilson at brunch whether it was usual for American audiences to applaud standing up. He said no, it was very unusual, and particularly in Boston.

What a kind man he is, like so many other tenderhearted Jews! He had arranged a special telephone call to Walton-on-Thames, as a surprise for Carol, so that she could talk to her family across the Atlantic!

Our aircraft left New Jersey at 5 o'clock (N.Y. time). It was an oily old DC-8. and carried us the 500 miles or so to Raleigh in about 2 hours at 14,000 feet. The afternoon was a hot haze and the dim country nearer to New York was chiefly remarkable to an Englishman for the almost invariably white houses. Incidentally, south of Boston the country is visibly populated! We began by passing over a flat chessboard plain dotted with these white dice, but presently came to a more bosky, savannalike, humpy country with rivers in it. I think we crossed the Potomac, the James River and the Roanoke. On our starboard side there were distant mountains, perhaps the foothills of the Appalachians? Eventually we came to the strange, gray, zebra-striped terraces of Raleigh.

On the whole, America is more wooded than not. At any rate, this coast is. I suppose the normal skin of the world is woodland. It is only where man settles that it becomes itchy, bald, and breaks out into the eczema patches of agriculture.

Nobody met us at Raleigh. There were no taxis. We were tired. When we rang up our sponsor to find out if we were expected at all, she asked me to take two classes and two meals with the faculty, apart from the lecture (and one class) specified in the contract. I was tired enough to refuse one of the classes. One of the reasons why I was grumpy was that I fancy this is a female college, which means rewriting the whole lecture. The lecture is called The Pleasures of Learning and deals with the education of males. Obviously women have to learn different skills.

The time in Raleigh is one hour earlier than it is in New York. The local accent is a delightful drawl. The main article of commerce in all the shops near this hotel seems to be parts of automobiles. The street is long and straight and rather featureless. The Negroes who are the hotel staff are plentiful and dressed in scarlet jackets. My bedroom is on the 10th floor, but not so grand as in New York. I am in a bad temper.

Carol has retired to wash her hair, and I am going to have a shower and go to bed and read *Beatniks.*

Our hotel is called the Sir Walter and has a large bust of Raleigh in the hall. He planted the first English colony on Roanoke Island in 1587 and the first white child born in America (Virginia Dare) was born there, but the whole colony had vanished when he returned. Also, in 1903, the Wright brothers made the first aerial flight fairly near here, at Kitty Hawk, and there is a mosaic of their airplane on the floor of the airport.

7 · 10 · 63

We presented ourselves in our own taxi at the college steps, feeling aggrieved that nobody had met or transported us, only to find that these were simple Episcopalian teachers who had probably been guessing that we would rather be left to ourselves, and had not been asked to meet us by the agents. The girls range from sixteen to twenty. Within a few moments of arrival the sponsor, Miss Morrison, had agreed to my changing the subject of the lecture to Hadrian (with slides). We lunched in the main hall, where the children sang to me:

All the visitors, all the visitors,
We are singing
Praises ringing
We will never find your equal
All the visitors, here's to you.

(At this I had to stand up and bow.)

After luncheon I sat for an hour and twenty minutes with a class of the elder girls, and we chatted about everything from Beatniks to Richard Burton and Elizabeth Taylor. They seemed content with it.

The head of the English Department, Mr. John Tate, kindly spent the rest of the afternoon driving us around Raleigh.

The population is 90,000, he said, with perhaps 10,000 of them Negroes. He is from Mississippi, yet is a strong anti-segregationalist. The attitude toward the problem, at least here, seems less extremist than they told us in Massachusetts and New York. He drove us around the Negro quarters, which are ill painted through the poverty of the inhabitants, but not as dilapidated as they will be when we get farther south.

Much of the wide, clear, flat, sunny city (noon temperature 82°) is in imitation Colonial architecture, very pleasant but not the real thing. There is little American Gothic.

He taught me to recognize dogwood trees. In the morning, on our own, we had heard grasshoppers (?) chirruping beautifully, and a long-tailed gray bird with rather dark cheeks like a shrike and a good song, and had photographed the pigeons bathing in a fountain.

The Hadrian lecture went moderately well in the evening and the reception, etc., kept us up till after midnight. There were about 400 in the audience, rather more than the usual number so far. I am becoming a "trouper" (counting the house, playing for laughs, complaining or boasting, as all actors do, that it is a good or bad audience).

The memorable facts about Raleigh were a) that Mrs. Tate (who invited us for dinner) cooked the most magnificent crabmeat flambé in scallop shells I have ever had—a bit like Coupe Jacques (?). The side dish was a pâté enclosed in clear marmite jelly. Our tour is jokingly known as the Chicken Circuit, because you are supposed to be fed exclusively on cold chicken salad, but we have not found it like this at all.

Another memorable fact was that I had been complaining of my ignorance about the birds and trees. In the evening I was waylaid by a wonderfully pretty girl of seventeen or so (Harriet Williams—remember to write to her) who had gone downtown of her own accord and bought me a useful illustrated bird book. I gave her a kiss, feeling rather like Leigh Hunt.

John Tate also introduced me to trees—dogwood, long-leaved pine, pecan and the Judas tree, all of which I can now recognize. Remember myrtle.

Incidentally, from the bird book, the singing stranger in the shrubs near the state house must have been either a mockingbird or a catbird or a loggerhead shrike. If we have time we will go back and identify it.

I was dead right about slavery and segregation! (Jokingly.) In the hall of this hotel there are ten very smart Negroes in scarlet jackets and gold lace and the domestic labor problem of New York does not exist. Tate says that one of the reasons why the South is so furiously segregationalist is because they don't want to lose the cheap labor. I said, well, perhaps it is because the Negro is only fitted for this sort of work? He replied, That is because they are denied education for other sorts.

The other argument is, Would you like your daughter to be married to one?

Tate's answer is that in the existing social conditions he would do everything in his power to dissuade her (because of the ostracism, etc., and the fate of the children, *not* because of the color, i.e. for social reasons, not racial ones) but that if she insisted he would submit. He added that all white women in the South are convinced they are going to be raped by the next Negro they meet, but that the prepotency of Negroes so far as he knows is largely a myth.

Out of the car window in the afternoon I found myself looking into the eyes of a beautiful Negro boy of about twelve, at an intersection. I looked upon him with admiration and affection, but he did not want to meet my gaze. His face went deadpan. Is this old white man wanting to rape me, lynch me, cut off my balls and make me eat them? (At some lynchings within living memory they did.) It was humiliating for me, and for the honor of my race I longed to get out of the car and give him a hug.

One good thing is that time is on our side. The statistics of lynching show that it is rarer and rarer, if not already extinct.

Tate says he expects a new explosion in Birmingham.

8 · 10 · 63

Last night the ushers wore long, white, bridal, organdy dresses like a party of Ophelias, so I was glad I had put on a tuxedo.

Before dinner, in the vivid sunset and strong stridulation of the crickets (?), I saw what would have been a nightjar in England—here, either a whippoorwill or a common nighthawk.

This morning we found a convention of the U.D.C. (United Daughters of the Confederacy) in the hotel and, while Carol wrote bread-and-butter letters, I went out to visit the supposed mockingbird. I got a good look at him on a lamppost but was none the wiser. Bird books are never much help—or one-dollar ones aren't. By the eye-stripe he ought to have been a loggerhead shrike, but do shrikes sing well? I was not close enough to see the bill.

Watched a male pigeon trying to interest a female in love, and reflected how many species there are in which the females simply don't have a clue about copulation.

Photographed some statues to Confederate and 1898 soldiers (To Our Confederate Dead, First at Bethel Last at Appomattox. The boy of 1898 was an ensign (First Fallen). I thought how shamefully little we know or care about American history.

There have been three Presidentes from North Carolina.

We covered the 130 miles to Charlotte in a super Electra at 11,000 feet, looking down on the strange variety of soils which underlie the woodlands of North Carolina. They vary capriciously from a sort of white clay through gray and brown to a rusty red of Devonshire in England—patches of all sorts like a mange in the tree-pelt of this part of America. We were met at the airport and driven by car into South Carolina. The two ladies who met us were in dark glasses, an insulting form of disguise generally adopted by people who have something to conceal, but they turned out to be bright and friendly. They stopped at a cotton field to pick me a boll of it, which I put in my buttonhole. Miss Williford told us that the last lynching she remembered was in Mississippi in 1959. Both ladies were antisegregation and said that there has not lately been trouble in Rock Hill, where we now are.

I am to address some 2,000 or 2,500 young ladies at Winthrop College tomorrow afternoon, with a microphone round my neck. This is the largest number of humans I have ever spoken to, except on radio or TV.

Tonight we have to go to a cocktail party at 8 o'clock.

Electronically (?) operated lift buttons will not work if I touch them with the rubber ferule of my walking stick.

Last night we ate a special grape called scuppernong. You pinch it so that it slides out of its skin into your mouth.

I found a "cricket" and it really is a cricket. It is brown and about three times as large as a grasshopper, but the mouth parts and wing structure are different from a grasshopper's, however much they resemble each other superficially. It belongs to a different order.

The cocktail party was successful, with goodwill on both sides. I tried to find out what sort of level I shall have to pitch my lecture at (this is the "Bible belt") but sufficient unto the day is the evil thereof.

Carol is a tower of strength, as usual.

Tired.

North Carolina was said to be "the valley of humiliation between two mountains of arrogance" (Virginia and South

Carolina). I asked why, and was told that socially speaking the two mountains thought themselves superior.

To bed.

I have agreed to take a class on Chaucer at 12:45. I must re-edit my notes on the Pleasures of Learning to suit a vast female audience at 4 P.M. Then dinner early. Then a reception at 6.

To bed, to bed, to bed.

9 · 10 · 63

In the aircraft yesterday I suddenly felt a twinge of active dislike for the burly Caucasians who surrounded us. They were too big, too blond, too jolly, too complacent, too obstinately sure of their own opinions. In other circumstances they might have been hefty Nazis, a bit too thick and pink and pimply, with yellow hairs on their chunky forearms and blunt fingers, their whole build more massive than mine. Perhaps I was jealous.

There moved among them as strong a Negro soldier, neatly dressed in the uniform of some airborne regiment, much more supple and sculpturally beautiful, but walking delicately like Agag and "keeping his eyes in the boat." His face was reserved and rather melancholy. The masculinity of us bullies made him move a bit like a woman, and he tripped in his great boots on the steps of the aircraft as if he had been wearing high heels.

I felt some of the same dislike this morning, walking round the sunny slopes of Rock Hill. It was plain we were in the Bible belt by the cheapness of the shopwindows, the vulgarity of their Draje-like furniture, the more than suburban cretonnes, the tin watches and glass jewelry, the artificial flowers and the perfectly horrible pictures selling for about 2 dollars framed. In one window, among sports accessories, there was an open, illustrated family Bible, hideously printed.

There is no *fun* in this, like the fun of Greenwich Village. It is more like those ghastly, enormous dwarfs at 181st Street.

To 2,100 of these people, but of the female sex, I have to give myself this afternoon, and I must do so with a will, remembering they are my brother humans who are doing their best.

The main article of commerce in the Carolinas seems to be automobiles. The shops which sell or service them or provide spare parts are more numerous than drugstores.

Opposite my hotel window on the sixth floor is an enormous pin oak (new tree for my list) which is as high as we are.

The class held at 1:45 was a success (on Chaucer).

A lecturer in my predicament can't help thinking of the old adage: "Two's Company, two thousand one hundred is none."

Now I must begin to eat humble pie about the South. All that grumbling in the last two pages was because I was scared stiff of having to talk about learning to such a quantity of unlearned women, while disbelieving in *male* learning for females.

However, I spent two or three hours rewriting the talk so that it was suitable, hung it on Richard Burton and Julie, and won something like an ovation—though not a standing one. They also begged me to come back next year!

We had dinner with the girls, then sat for an hour at a very pleasant reception, then, over and above the bargain (as my Chaucer talk was), went on to a series of readings from Ibsen which were held in a smaller, intimate theatre.

The readings were done in costume, with simple scenery and lighting, and were done remarkably well. Ibsen in a Southern drawl is revealing—it becomes something of a dialect play, which somehow helps the Scandinavianess of it. The final excerpt was from *Peer Gynt,* the death of Asa, and this in the accent of South Carolina made vivid the likeness between Tennessee Williams and Ibsen. In fact, it might have been a piece out of *Hot Tin Roof.* I had not thought of this before, i.e. that Williams is a direct continuation of Ibsen.

At the reception we had a lot of conversation about everything under the sun, including the difference between North and South (we did not mention segregation). In the North I had been warned that the people of the South were not wicked, just stupid! I asked these Southern lassies themselves what the difference was, and got a revealing answer.

The North, they said, is more interested in Causes, while we are lazy and only interested in People. And, they added with touching candor, the people in the North are brighter than we are intellectually.

How could I go on feeling meanly about them after this?

It is true that their two wonderful theatres (one seating 2,500 and the other 400) are too little used. At Williams College there would be a queue of juvenile directors, actors and playwrites waiting for the use of each theatre practically every week. It is true that this not enormous town is more or less "out in the sticks"—they said so themselves. But nothing could have been warmer or more receptive than the welcome they gave to this particular bringer of culture.

The campus as a whole is not particularly interesting architecturally, but the hallway outside the smaller theatre is an enchanting imitation of the colonial sort of design which one associates with Scarlett O'Hara. The polished wooden floor there is magnificent.

The girls seemed to like me as much as I loved them, and two or three are coming to take us out tomorrow morning, before we have to leave for Washington.

It is the first time I have spoken with a microphone round my neck. You feel like a horse—hobbled and tethered on the lone prairie of that boundless and empty stage.

Carol tells me we are at the end of comparative freedom. After Washington it will be practically one-night stands.

I want to see and love America. I want to learn more from and about them than they can learn from me. It is going to be more difficult as we become more tired and more rushed by the schedule. But the more we give, the more we will get. In future I will try never to refuse anything we are asked to do.

One of the oddities of Rock Hill, not seen before now by us, is the strange stained glass of the church and Masonic windows, which look like thin slides of grayish horn from outside. This I must photograph tomorrow.

I think it is grasshoppers we hear by day, crickets by night. When the wind blows in the pin oaks the grasshoppers fall silent. I wish I could hear some frogs, or see a skunk or a coon.

10 · 10 · 63

At 13,000 ft. in a Super Electra above the sunny, brick-dust soil of South Carolina.

This morning four of the college girls took Carol to see over their campus and dormitory, dropping me off at a small park to look at birds and trees. Unfortunately the bird book was packed, but I did find for sure some mockingbirds, catbirds (which had a kind of *miawl*), a dun kind of woodpecker (yellow-shafted flicker?) blue jays and a cardinal. There was also a small bird rather bigger than a great tit with dark head, light breast and a cry like "sweep." (Phoebe?) I ate the acorn of one of their oaks and the nut of a hickory.

There was a fountain in the park. America so far is rather poor in public fountains and very poor in naked public statues. American statues tend to wear Federal or Confederate uniforms, with sabers, except if they are Washington, who was rather a natty dresser.

The girls finally drove us to the airport, after a breakdown of college transport, and talked en route a great deal about segregation. They feel bitterly about Northern criticism—the scars of the bloody Civil War have hardly healed—and asked pathetically whether the North was not being unfair to them? They pointed out that they had all been brought up by black mammies themselves. They said that they had *no* revulsion from colored people on account of color or smell or anything else. They said they did *not* think: Negroes were an inferior race in natural skills or culture (as, for instance, I think the Irish are to the English). They were all four antisegregation. I got the impression that Southerners who favor segregation may be doing so mainly out of obstinacy against the North. The Civil War was horribly bloody. Some river I have read of ran red with blood for several days, and more young Americans were killed than in all their wars since, added together. It is fairly recent history by European standards and the postwar settlement kept the South down, so one of the girls claimed, till about 1940.

They said that many slaves had wanted to go on being slaves, and this I believe. I promised to tell the North to stop nagging.

Now we are off to Washington for a last weekend of comparative freedom. So much to see, so little time.

The two main things I want to investigate in the capital are a) Jefferson, who, I now gather, was an architect like Hadrian; and b) the Smithsonian.

Smithsonian was an Englishman who left his money to America, to be spent on Culture—an amount which might now be equivalent to two or three million pounds. But the interesting thing is that he was an illegitimate Englishman, the supposed son of a Duke of Northumberland. He also had some relationship to Horace Walpole's "proud duke of Somerset." When I get home I must look him up, to see if he is mentioned in Walpole. I seem to remember that for some time the Northumberland surname, descending through the female line, was not Percy but Smith—hence the illegitimate Smith-son.

I am glad to think that a noble English bastard was responsible for half the culture in the capital of the U.S.A.

The Washington Monument is realy stunning. You feel you could balance Nelson's Column on the tip as a lightning conductor without noticing it. It is 555 feet high. I used to maneuver airplanes at 400 ft. with a margin of safety.

Washington was purposefully built to be magnificent and opulent and the capital of the greatest country in the world. It is fashionable among envious people to sneer about its architecture. But its chalk-white domes and columns and its wide avenues *are* magnificent and opulent, and if its architecture is not a servile copy of Greek or Roman or Palladian, well, it is all the *better* for not being a copy.

It is a variation. Hurrah!

The Negro porter at our hotel in Rock Hill (the Andrew Jackson) discussed the cost of living in England and America this morning. "Well," he said, "Ah guess it's all about the same. Yew cain't get rich nowhere."

Carol says that the girls had painted the lavatory seat in their dormitory a phosphorescent blue and put two eyes over the toilet roll which also glowed in the dark. I hope this will not be bad for their health.

American airlines use *Spanish* as the alternative language for their notices, just as the English use French for NE PAS SE PENCHER EN DEHORS.

We have recrossed a time boundary and put our watches back to New York time.

11 · 10 · 63

We only have three clear days in Washington—incidentally, we are at a Roger Smith hotel again, as cheap and yet as luxurious (for the money) as the one we poor Europeans had in New York. It is difficult to decide what to do, with such an *embarras de richesses* spread before us. It will take 3 hours each way to visit Monticello and the University of Virginia in a bus. We must just treat ourselves as tourists and pick tours.

One of the chief English sneers against Americans in Europe is about their "tourism"—their cameras and guided tours and "doing" Florence, etc., in a day. I will never sneer this sneer again. They are only in Europe for a certain length of time—and much credit to them for bothering to come so far in search of culture. They want to "take in" all they can. So do Carol and I in America. We are tied hand and foot to our lecture schedule and yet we want to love and understand this colossal country. What other solution is there, except to take guided tours? (Next time we will stay in one place for a long time. Two of my sponsors have already written to ask us back to lecture again, and one has offered a job teaching.)

Lecturing. I had to make a horrid confession to Carol last night. I am beginning to *enjoy* these lectures, to enjoy having more than 2,000 people in the hollow of my hand. What a ham! I might as well be Richard Burton himself, and I am not ashamed of it. It is a minor art. I am actually looking forward to the next lecture (at first I was shaking like a leaf) and wanting to charm, to control, to play on, to compel the expected laugh. I have even begun to be interested in timing!

One evening when I was being too fulsome in my praise, Father Shea said to me cheerfully, "Stop condescending to us poor Americans." I must be careful of this. Too much praise can be an insult.

Well, we are tired but triumphant. We took a tour called Bi and were hustled round the White House, a waxworks exhibition, the Bureau of Printing and Engraving, and part of the Smithsonian. At this point we branched off on our own account, went up the Washington Monument and came home for a shower. It was a beautifully hot day of Indian Summer.

First we passed the old Ford Theatre where Lincoln was assassinated. The interesting thing about this was that the play itself, which was in its 1001st performance, was instantly suppressed and has never been performed since. It was called *Our American Cousin*. Strange. Look at it from the author's point of view. Booth seems to have killed more than one person.

The White House can be visited for two hours every morning and Buckingham Palace can not. It is clean, it is lived in, it is fairly impressive and it is very rightly given its name. (Indeed, Washington might well be called the White Town —I made up a line like the famous one about Petra: "The chalk-white city half in love with Time.") President Kennedy's wife has given to at least one of the rooms a slight air of an enlarged Malmaison. But on the whole, for so grand a continent, the furniture and paintings are second rate and the whole thing has too much the feeling of an expensive hotel. There is nothing royal about it, nothing princely, not even anything particularly elegant or valuable. It is just a well-washed public mansion, not palatial and not particularly American.

Fortunately the columns on the lawn front have elongated themselves. There seems to be something elongating in the air of America—its redwood trees, its skyscrapers and its classical columns.

The waxworks were excellent, a worthy continuation of the Chamber of Horrors and the rest of Madame Tussaud's.

My new flash attachment failed to function here on the camera, sending me into a renewed rage against electricians. I had to buy rather poor postcards and even then there were none taken of the best tableaux.

My rage was not calmed by the Bureau for printing dollar bills. It was without exception the most fatuous tour I have ever made in my life. Who wants to see dollar bills printed? Why not watch them printing lavatory paper? Large parties of us sheep were assembled in tardy batches, queued, kept waiting, tediously led down horrible sick-green prisonlike corridors with cast-iron pillars and hundreds of twopenny Stars-and-Stripes, herded into ugly elevators, lectured by colored female guides, treated with the delays of a half-dead bureaucracy—and all to gawp at a lot of out-of-date machinery flapping pieces of paper. The worship of the dollar indeed! Can the rest of the party possibly have enjoyed it, and if not why did they submit? I didn't. After the first hall I insisted on being let out of the queue and sent back to the entrance against the stream of visitors, thus, I hope, disorganizing the entire production line of the Treasury of the United States.

Carol continued on the conveyer belt while I smoked a pipe outside.

The Smithsonian and the Washington Monument made up for everything.

The original building of the Smithsonian is a red or chocolate-colored joke straight out of the Castle of Otranto for dam, as sired by some English Victorian lunatic asylum. *Unfortunately* it is not particularly American: it is *not* American Gothic, but a melee of Horry Walpole and Sir Giles Gilbert Scott. Yet it is a wonderfully funny structure. Parts of it have crossed the Brighton Pavilion with a skating rink or a seaside pier, and some administrator of sardonic genius has arranged that the latest rockets from Cape Canaveral should be erected among its pleasure domes and the walls and towers that gird it round. The missiles are indistinguishable from the minarets.

The ensemble is a late-Victorian nightmare of Kubla Khan, with flashes of Science Fiction. I fell in love with it at once, though I could not help wishing it had been less English.

There is no statue of Smithson that I could find, yet a taxi driver told us he is buried there, not having visited America while alive.

The Washington Monument.

Really, it is breathtaking.

Five hundred and fifty-five feet, 50 landings, 898 steps, all of *nothing*—not of flats, not of offices, not of anything useful or habitable, just sheer art. I think it is magnificent that a nation should take such trouble, should pour out so much treasure, on an object that is completely useless except as beauty. They talk of Americans as being materialists. They are the most idealistic nation on earth.

The very rapid elevator takes 70 seconds to get to the top, from where I photographed all Washington with my telescopic lens, without one twinge of acrophobia. Too interested.

The monument was discussed in 1783, begun in 1848, finished in 1884. It cost $1,187,710.31. It weighs 90,854 tons—more than the *Queen Elizabeth.*

Carol walked down all the steps from the top and says that there are stones set inside from forty-nine states of the Union and from the ruins of Carthage, Brazil, Japan, Greece and Turkey.

I must not say this out loud, but what a closed, obstinate, unpleasant face George Washington had. His portraits are everywhere.

He designed the original Stars-and-Stripes with a lady called Betsy Ross. She persuaded him to have a five-pointed star instead of a six-pointed one "because she could cut it out with a single snip of her scissors." I cannot understand the mechanics of this.

You can tell a new Stars-and-Stripes from an old one, now that we have fifty states, by a glance at the arrangement of the stars. They come in fives and fours.

Carol says that although the base of the obelisk is much wider than the top (about 55 ft. against 34 ft.) yet the steps inside are narrower at the bottom than the top. When you think it over, this is an obvious necessity of engineering. The bottom needs a more solid mass of masonry than the top.

Remember to mention this in the Hadrian lecture. His famous dome on the Pantheon is of pumice at the top, for lightness. The thickness of the walls of Robert Mills' obelisk (he was the final architect of the Washington Monument) is 15 feet at the base, but only 18 inches at the top of the shaft.

How often does this edifice get struck by lightning? What wonder of the world, what Colossus of Rhodes or Pharos of Alexandria is comparable to it?

It presses the earth beneath it with a weight of nine tons to the square inch!

There was only one sensible question to ask our guide at that horrible dollar-printing establishment. How did the automatic machine on our Hudson River train to Albany test the dollar bills it gave change for? I asked it. She did not know the answer.

While I was smoking my pipe on the steps, a mourning dove flew by. At any rate it was a very thin-looking pigeon! (Doves also get elongated.)

It used to be fashionable among English architects to sneer at the Washington Monument for being too big—like making a candlestick twenty feet high. This is pure nonsense and a misleading analogy. Why shouldn't it be big? *It is not a candlestick.*

I fear that the Americans have been talked into being ashamed of the old Smithsonian, just as I in my youth was talked into despising the delightful Albert Memorial in London. It has proved impossible to find a postcard of it so far.

After our long, dusty travels and observations (and writing this) we had a splendid meal at the hotel. It was fresh, delicious, abundant, and not more costly than in England. I had a large mixture of iced fruits like melon, Southern-fried half chicken with baked potato, crisp salad with that cheese dressing (limburger?) and a huge slice of lemon meringue pie with two cups of coffee. There were also hot garlic rolls and butter. Everything was impressively served and came to about $3.75. Carol's, which included an enormous steak, was a few cents more expensive. The dressing she chose for her salad was Thousand Island.

Now I am going to put up my swollen, aching, hard-pressed old feet and go to bed and look at television.

How the young architect Major Pierre l'Enfant, whose vision of Washington was left to limp and falter for almost a hundred years (even Mills' obelisk was abandoned for 25 years at the height of 153 ft.), how proud he would be to see it now! The basis of the whole grand design is the French broadness of his avenues.

12 · 10 · 63

Because the ladies at Colston Leigh's did not bother to have us met at Raleigh (although it was offered in the contract), and because the Hadrian lecture was the first time through and the gentleman operating the projector could not hear what I said, and because I was too tired to take an extra class for Miss Morrison (which was not in the contract), the ladies in question have written edgy letters to each other and to me. I was too late to stop Carol answering.

Well, we are gluttons for punishment. I calculate we voluntarily covered about 310 miles today in a bus, purely to "take in" Jefferson, and we were wonderfully rewarded. We crossed and recrossed a time line.

First there was the three-hour run in the bus, which gave us a much better idea of Virginia than we had had by flying over it. Behind us there was a lady addressing her husband like a public meeting, and I reflected that I ought to pay more attention to the various sorts of American accents. When I lived in Ireland, I could easily distinguish between the accents of the North, Dublin, Galway and Cork. I also reflected that some American ladies seem to have developed scraggy bosoms, for which their husbands have compensated by developing huge, female, Dutch behinds.

An English visitor begins to notice odd characteristics. The Americans are much less inhibited about their beautiful flag than the English are, and they display it much more. A Washington shop called Julius Garfield [sic] had five flags over each entrance, which did not seem particularly unusual for Washington. Incidentally, both the Union Jack and the Stars-and-Stripes are geometrical flags (not heraldic like the English royal ensign) and they are all the more vivid for that. Geometrical flags ripple more. But they must, as in America, be clean.

You are struck by the many churches in America, and by

the fact that they are used. You also notice that American housewives like to have ornamental artificial flamingos in their gardens, as the English have toadstools and dwarfs. It is needless to say that everywhere (and illuminated by night) there are millions of advertisements and trillions of automobiles, in junk heaps, on sale secondhand, or in use. The signs are for everything from Motels (Vacancy in red) to Dunked Donuts. I like them. I admired the vast autobahns along which we sped. My theory (due to flying in last time from Newfoundland) that nobody lives in America is incorrect. For dozens of miles around Washington there are dormitory townships for commuters.

"Antiques" in America are touching. Everything over 25 years old seems to count as one.

We noticed that it is impossible to photograph the Washington monument from any angle. It is too vast. You can't get in the tiny ants of people at its base, and the lovely circle of flags there, as well as its own prodigiousness. We also wondered what would happen to a war if you dropped quite a small bomb on the Pentagon. For that matter, it would probably be better to leave it standing. All those acres of bureaucracy ought to succeed in losing any war. We observed too that Arlington is for living soldiers as well as for dead ones.

The long, long journey made me think of poor Lolita, endlessly driven from motel to motel. I hope my eighteen-year-old Carol is not suffering the same miseries as she did.

As we got farther south I saw many buzzards (or could they have been turkey vultures? They held their wings above the horizontal line). I noticed how little visible agriculture there was. What do farmers do, except for Indian corn and tobacco? Compared with England, there were few cattle or horses, and little market gardening. We did pass stalls of pumpkins. I suppose all the wheat, etc., is grown more economically in the middle of the continent.

But all the time, we were ignorantly traversing the country of the Civil War. I really must learn more about the bitterness of this than is to be gathered from the rubbish in *Gone With the Wind.*

We were crossing battlefields. At some point near Manassas we must have crossed Bull Run, the river which flowed with blood for days. At Warrenton there was a gift shop still flying the Confederate flag. At another place they were advertising the rifles of those old slaughters for sale. In a wide field we saw some lonely cannon.

And we were getting among the segregationalists. Our cabdriver at Charlottesville was a young, friendly, hospitable, handsome person who took endless trouble for us and kept down his charges. Yet he talked without remorse of "whipping" the Negroes and was a violent segregationalist. He said that last month at Charlottesville there had been a colored attempt to get service in a restaurant by a sort of sit-down strike. "So we whipped a couple, aind it paist over." He drove us to photograph a Negro shack, which I did with shame in my heart while the darkies on the porch covered their heads or tried to get out of the picture. At the bus station, there was a slightly more shabby inner compartment where they had to eat by themselves. On the bus itself, they did not have separate seats.

"Aire caib company haid to take on two Negro drivers by law, so we leuked aout for *any* reason to fire them. We got one because his wheels churned up some graivel on the drive of a house while he was backing."

Yet this was a perfectly pleasant young man who took an interest in us, invited us back, was flattered by our interest in his town, addressed us as Yew-all, and was happily proud of his local celebrity Thomas Jefferson—who wrote "We hold these truths to be self-evident, that all men are created equal."

This brings me to the object of the expedition, and I don't know where to begin.

In the first place, my beloved Hadrian. Jefferson was a *peaceful* ruler, like him. He doubled the size of America by purchase, not by war. He reestablished the Library of Congress, where I am one day to speak. Like Hadrian, he hated titles and would not be called "Your Excellency."

But the parallels are eerie. Both men were tall, athletic, musical, cultured, and I even have a vague idea that Hadrian had sandy hair like Jefferson. Both were brilliant practical architects. Both had universal interests. Jefferson could "calculate an eclipse, survey an estate, tie an artery, plan an edifice, try a cause, break a horse, dance a minuet and play the violin." (Hadrian's instrument was the flute.) Both had an enormous influence, as great as Christopher Wren's, on the buildings of their country. Neither could reply to abuse. Both were noted for their scholarship. Each might have been the subject of my lecture called The Pleasures of Learning, and "had a habit of learning from everyone anything worth cultivating."

President Kennedy once spoke to a grand dinner of artists and scientists. "I think," said he, "this is the most extraordinary collection of talent, of human knowledge, that has ever been gathered together at the White House—with the possible exception of when Thomas Jefferson dined here alone."

Well, but the wonderful surprise was saved for the end of our trip, when, after Monticello, we rushed round the University of Virginia, which Jefferson established and designed and was the first president of.

The great Rotunda, completed in 1826 to Jefferson's plans, is practically a copy of Hadrian's greatest building, the Pantheon at Rome.

I was mooching about in it, in my dumb way, when I noticed from a plan on the wall that the height to the dome was the same as the diameter. (It is so at the Pantheon.) I pointed this out to the undergraduate guide, who led us at once to a photograph of the Pantheon itself! (Unfortunately, Jefferson's building has windows. I wonder if he put them there himself? There was a fire in 1895 and the whole has been pawed over by an architect called Stanford White, who replaced Jefferson's double columns with single ones.)

The fire makes a stirring saga.

The ponderous marble statue of Jefferson used to stand on the second-floor balcony. During the fire, while the wives of the faculty carried out the library books in their aprons, the undergraduates contrived to knock down the statue so that it fell on a table (only breaking off the edges of the frock coat and the table itself) and to convey it in a blanket down a narrow curving staircase and to roll it down the long back steps to the lawn. Nobody knows how they found the strength to do this.

The statue is packed with poetry in yet another way.

There is a secret society of alumni at Virginia University which is called the Seven. Nobody knows who they are. They exist to do good. Their post office is the pedestal of the statue. Any letter addressed to them can be left at Jefferson's marble feet and sooner or later it disappears. It is supposed that they have a key of the building and can get in at night. Their secret sign is painted on the pavement outside, at the foot of another statue.

The architecture of Jefferson's splendid buildings is a sort of Williamsburg Palladian, i.e. it is a sort of Roman Classical carried out with white pillars, pediments, etc., and red brick, which gives it a look of Queen Anne or William and Mary. (Jefferson was educated at Williamsburg.) Unfortunately it has hardly any American characteristics—but at least it was carried out in the style then almost contemporary in England. (1819, but conservative for that date.)

This brings me back to Monticello, the charming country house to which the old President retired, as Hadrian retired to his inner sanctum at the Villa Tibur. Monticello is in the same Anne style as his University.

Like Hadrian, he had built it himself. Like Hadrian, he wanted domestic privacy for his old age after a lifetime of public service. Like Hadrian, he was an inventive and slightly eccentric man. (Hadrian was the first bearded emperor and Jefferson would not have stairways more than 24 inches broad, saying that they wasted space and lowered internal temperatures.)

We went over the little, comfortable, family villa (lots of grandchildren on the upper floors) and admired its dodges—

the revolving chair, the camera obscura, the octagonal filing table, the two-foot stairways, the seven-day clock, the copying machine for writing two letters at once, the bed in a party wall so that he could get out of it into a study on the one side or a living room on the other, and the wind vane on the roof. Jefferson liked to keep a record of wind and temperature, so I took a reading of the wind for him on our visit. It was E.N.E.—a glorious, sunny day.

The old gentleman (he was not a soldier like Hadrian) had leveled the 857-ft.-high hilltop to build his home and command its superb views of the Blue Mountains. I am glad to say they let him be buried there. He died on the exact 50th anniversary of the Declaration of Independence.

Hadrian long refused all titles except the academic and artistic one of Archon of Athens.

Jefferson, who had drafted and signed the Declaration of Independence, did not mention on his tombstone that he had been the President of America. He wrote that he was the father of the University of Virginia.

Well, God bless him. We have had a very happy day.

13 · 10 · 63

At breakfast I tried tearing five-pointed stars out of the Sunday paper. I cannot discover how to do this in one operation.

Afterwards we paid a duty visit to the Jefferson Memorial, because we loved him.

Its white monopteron with portico is American all right (designed by John Russell Pope and the survivors of his firm, Otto P. Eggers and Daniel P. Higgins) and it is impressive and beautifully situated, but it would not have given much pleasure to Jefferson or Hadrian. Its diameter is not equal to its height, its columns are out of proportion, it is not lit by a hole in the dome, and the portico is too protrusive for the ideas of Pantheon or Virginia. Never mind. It is more "American" than anything in Virginia University or Rome.

Bits I left out of yesterday's scrapbook:

Monticello is domed like the Rotunda.

The dome of the Rotunda used to have movable stars in it, which could be moved seasonally, rather like a planetarium.

Nude statues seem to be taboo in America. Even fig leaves have to be replaced with swirls of drapery. Jefferson had a statue of Ariadne in his hall, but she is swathed from head to foot. For some mysterious reason a small pinch of the stone material has been carefully pulled aside to expose about a handbreadth—of her navel!

There is a new fashion in electric light bulbs on chandeliers. They are blown in a flame shape, like candle flames.

After meals you eat a couple of peppermints.

Aircraft landing at Washington International gives the same fright that you get at Boston. You seem to be landing in the Potomac.

One day an aircraft is going to run into the Washington Obelisk, just as one already has into the Empire State. I shall be sorrier for the lovely obelisk than for the victims.

The main public design of this great city is a compass.

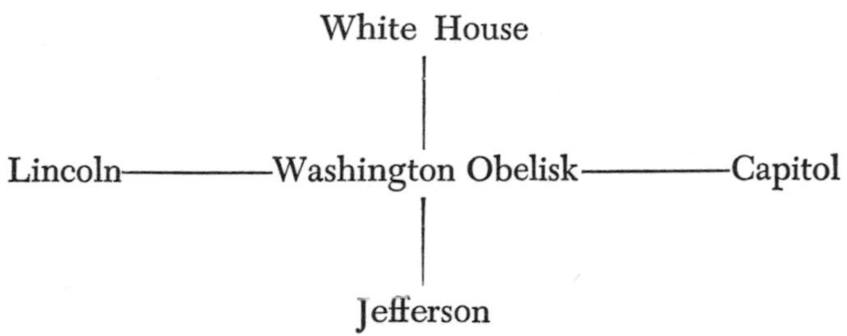

Carol washed her hair this afternoon, so I took a taxi to the waxworks (with a new flashgun) via the outside of the Capitol, which I photographed from the side, not front. I was out of the cab about sixty seconds.

The cabdriver, a cantankerous old gentleman, gave me his views about segregation. He did not want to associate with colored people and he said they did not want to associate with him. He does not stop for colored fares at night. He claimed that they were liable to murder taxi drivers. He refused to wait for me at the waxworks, where I only wanted a few minutes to take three flashes, and proceeded to swindle me hatefully over the fare. He charged $3.70, which I was too ignorant to dispute. The return fare in another taxi was 70 cents.

In the waxworks I longed to buy myself a gilded shield with the American escutcheon. It should be an eagle displayed, or, clutching a thunderbolt and a sheaf of arrows, on an azure ground, with a tinctured shield of the national flag on its breast and the motto *E Pluribus Unum.* But it cost 25 dollars, which I could not afford on myself.

I searched in vain for some cuff links for Carol, but they all had Washington written on them in a vulgar script.

There is some (little) truth in what the driver said. If agitators like Luther King did not stir them up, the Negroes *might* remain passive in their not very irksome divorce from the whites. Probably it is more an economic struggle than a racial one.

On the whole, the educated classes (University faculties, etc.) are against segregation, and the cabdriver classes are for it. So far as we have seen, Negroes are separated in no buses or shops and very few eating counters at drugstores. (In this excellent hotel there is no discrimination whatever.) They keep to themselves in a way which seems voluntary, as the driver said, but wouldn't you keep to yourself if you had been treated like a dog for two hundred years? (N.B. Dogs are rather well treated.)

This particular driver claimed that Negroes were by nature inferior and ineducable to his level.

He looked as unpleasant as George Washington and resembled him facially.

Incidentally, it was dear Jefferson who stopped the importation of slaves into Virginia.

15 · 10 · 63

This is a bad week for the diary. So much lecturing and sightseeing and so many classes. For instance, yesterday, for which there is no entry, ended at 1 A.M. after a swim in the college pool at West Virginia Wesleyan (Buckhannon).

I just get time to scribble a note in my pocket book now and then, and here copy them out during a free hour between classes. Incidentally the lectures, etc., are going with a bang. Today, at Elkins, I got something like an ovation from a mixed compulsory captive audience of 400, who were likely to be more interested in the girls beside them than in me—particularly as the acoustics were awful.

Well, on the 14th we flew from Washington International by Lake Central Air Line—in an ancient unpressurized DC-3, what the English call a Dakota, which made our ears ache a little—to a lovely little airport called Elkins in West Virginia. It was hardly bigger than the airport at Alderney, though it did have a proper runway. We flew in this still-glorious weather at about the ceiling of the Moths I used to fly, via Martinsburg, where we landed en route. Let's guess the distance as about two hundred miles? Nearer to Washington there were plenty of houses and townships below us, looking down on the white towers of which I opined that American architecture is essentially monumental. We crossed the Blue Ridge Mountains and the beautiful Shenandoah Valley—which, despite the sea-chantey, has nothing to do with the sea. Near Martinsburg had been fought the battle of Antietam, in fairly open country of yellow and gray soil. (It must have been difficult for generals to organize satisfactory battles in the wooded country to the east.) As we penetrated more and more into the Alleghenies the land grew emptier again, till we were passing over the forest ridges about two and a half thousand feet high, or perhaps three thousand, over the lost lonely timbered mountains where

Rip Van Winkle might still have been able to sleep undisturbed.

We were met by Mr. James Stansbury, a charming, intelligent, athletic person who assured us that we were really among the hillbillies in "West–by God–Virginia." West Virginians are proud of not being Virginians, were on the Federal side in the Civil War, or rather, 29,000 fought on the Union side and 8,000 fought for the Confederates, were among the first integrated, and are fond of saying to those who confuse them with the more lowland state that they are *West* (by God) Virginians. Mrs. Stansbury used to be nicknamed "Hoopie" at school and once took off her shoes there, in defiance, to show that hillbillies really did go barefoot.

Stansbury took us on quite a tour of the dirt roads and wooden houses to take photographs, showed us the gray timber houses, the once *brick* streets of Buckhannon, also a Tree of Heaven (or stink tree) and a huge car graveyard which had somehow established itself in these highlands. If the Americans *will* manufacture a billion cars a minute and have two or three in each family they must have somewhere to put the old ones. America gives the impression of having more cars in it than people. There is a local law that these immense funeral piles of automobiles must have an eight-foot fence around them to prevent the eyesore, but this is quite useless in a land of hillsides where eight feet hides nothing.

The classes and lecture and banquet are a haze to me already, except that they were happily received, but the hospitality and friendliness of both faculty and pupils is not a haze. Also, what is not a haze is the immense movement toward culture and grace which even these backwoods colleges have achieved. There really is a Renaissance going on in America and everybody was rightly proud of the music rooms (with Stereo sound) and the recreation rooms of the community center and the luxurious swimming pool in which we swam after a meeting to which 400 volunteers turned up and were enthusiastic. I played bowls, i.e. rolled two or three, for the first time in my life, in a magnificent alley, admired the billiard tables, postage system, etc., and ended up with half a dozen of the faculty at a dinner where I was taught to make a doll out of corn husks (another skill!). At this dinner there was also the college football team, great hunks of cheesecake with not unfriendly but defensive eyes.

We got back late to the motel—my first motel—I don't particularly care for them—and had to rise early this morning, to be motored to Elkins (Davis & Elkins College) at 8 A.M. by Dr. Williams. While having coffee in a restaurant and waiting for Dr. Williams, I had a conversation with a divorced truck driver who had custody of his only son.

A millionaire "wildcatter" called M. L. Benedum was a benefactor of both these colleges. A wildcatter is a prospector for oil among the wildcats (real) of these and other unpopulated uplands. His only son died and there was nothing for it but to leave his money in benefactions.

Elkins, where we now are in another motel, was founded by two "robber barons"—a member of the faculty so described them—who were senators and built their homes here. The homes were the two first buildings of the college. They, and the comical porter's lodge in American Bavarian, are the best *American* architecture locally, but at present they are unappreciated and you can't get postcards of them. The two senators were called Davis and Elkins. There is a good equestrian statue of Henry Gassaway Davis.

I had a Negro in my class this morning.

An illustrated book about American colleges ought to have a great many pictures of such a place as Williams, but also a great many of such a one as Elkins.

In the afternoon, Dr. Williams took us for a long drive through the backwoods valleys, where we photographed the old rough-hewn barns and houses of farmers, moonlighters or poor whites. "Moonlighters" are people with dual occupation: they are doing one job by day and another by moonlight. He was kind and patient with us, giving a running commentary on what we wanted to know.

I miss very much not being able to get into these woods, away from the highways, and see things like skunks and coons and rattlesnakes and cottonmouths. All of the wild life I have seen in West Virginia was a dead possum in our headlights on the road last night.

Benedum gave more ($400,000) to the Wesleyans than to Elkins—the Presbyterians are poor here and the Wesleyans are rich, because there are more of the latter—and the community center of the former is consequently grander. But even Elkins is far and away more luxurious than my last memory of Cambridge in England. Buckhannon (W. Virginia Wesleyan College) has a post office, lockers, game room, bowling alleys, bookstore, Olympic swimming pool, reading room, music listening rooms, conference room, F.M. radio station to open later, offices, coffee shop and lounge, private dining room, faculty lounge, social hall and a sort of roof garden terrace—all in the Community Center.

Everybody is humbly proud of this and delighted by my admiration.

11:30. Very successful lecture. Everybody enchanting. Very tired. We have been as happy among the so-called hill-billies as anywhere else, if not happier. They urged us to come back.

16 · 10 · 63

The economy of the Alleghenies, such as it was, was founded on coal mining, and timber, but here in the forest hills you think more of the Seneca Indians (we are on the Seneca Trail) who oppressed the Mingo's, or of the equally ferocious Shawnees. You also have to think of the hunters who are all about us at the moment, the Squirrel Season having opened while we are here. Lost in the vast tangle-wood, they are busy trying to destroy squirrels, grouse, turkey and deer (with the bow only—their gun season opens later). One deer was killed yesterday with the bow, out of 259 seen on Cheat Mountain, and the newspaper says, perhaps with a misprint, that 18 bear were shot. 621 of the 1,894 squirrels encountered were executed.

They begin trapping beavers in January.

We are surrounded by 115 hills higher than 4,000 ft., our temperature has varied between 80° and 32° (at night).

This is a week of despair for me and my diary—getting up early, flying too high in the haze, hardly time to make the acquaintance of our hosts, and seeing nothing of all the wonders.

We left Elkins in another Dakota and zigzagged to Pittsburgh, sneaking into valleys on the way to make three stops at small airdromes (one named after Benedum). The car cemeteries, even in these out-of-the-way places, are more conspicuous from the air than the human ones. At one point we flew through the high smoke of a forest fire. Our only memory of Pittsburgh, which we would have longed to see, was being charged the equivalent of 14/- for two ham sandwiches and two Cokes.

From there it was a T.W.A. super-G Constellation, radar equipped, at eleven thousand feet with the earth too hazy to be watched.

What is heartbreaking is that we are passing over or near such memorable scenes as that of Gettysburg (where the battle lasted 3 days) and Valley Forge where Washington almost lost the winter war against the British by the desertion of his army, and Winterthur where the famous house of a hundred rooms is, each furnished according to period. We are passing over the Mennonites and Amish, whose men wear beards and won't use cars or machinery. I have a vague recollection that they won't even wear buttons.

In Philadelphia itself we shall have no time for Independence Hall, where the Declaration of Liberty was signed, nor for the Liberty Bell, nor the symphony orchestra, nor Benjamin Franklin, nor the only cricket club in America, nor the Betsy Ross House where that famous flag was stitched whose 5-pointed stars are still puzzling me. It was made out of strips of petticoat and flannel.

We are passing the German and Dutch and Quaker part of America—all lost to us, because what is not flying is lecture or reception and actually (tomorrow) we are rising at 5 A.M. to catch our connection.

I don't care for these constellations—their three small tail-fins and somehow fishlike fuselage. But they are sumptuous inside. I reckon today we shall have covered 420 miles.

17 · 10 · 63

A brief and tired 20 minutes to get the diary a little up to date before the next engagement. It does take it out of you to be giving out all the time, autographing, having the hem of your garment touched and trying to charm the hearts of 400 at a time. Every audience has been as different as people are different, and treated as such.

We flew into the wide city of Philadelphia on the sunny islanded banks of the mighty Delaware, drove like mad to the hotel (no time for a shower) and were at a faculty reception by 6 P.M.

Our impressions of Philadelphia are horribly bounded by about twelve hours of mostly darkness, for we had to rise and leave again before dawn.

One visible thing noted. There is a huge and graceful bridge named after Walt Whitman. Where is there a bridge in London named after Shakespeare himself? These people are more cultured than we are.

The lecture on Hadrian went better than it deserved, after which Professor Setton took us over the magnificent library of the University (1,000,000 volumes) and entertained us in the Librarian's Room. It is heavily and grandly furnished, reminding me a little of the Laurentian Library in Florence. On its upper balcony were four busts. I walked as straight as a setting dog to one of them, saying, "There is Antinous." Nobody knew it, and nothing was written on it, but it was—and I had just been talking about him. How lovely to have hunted and found the memories of Hadrian from Naples to Philadelphia!

We stayed talking in the library till midnight, admired the Medici MSS which they have just bought for 40,000 dollars, and were invited for a private visit by the Settons, after the tour is over. Incidentally, the whole library remains open to students *till midnight!* I tried vainly to imagine the Cambridge University library condescending to do this. There is a real renaissance in America.

It was fine to sink back into the academic atmosphere and to converse with people who could also read medieval abbreviated Latin MSS.

How different each stop has proved to be!

This morning a United Airlines Viscount carried us to Buffalo at 300 m.p.h. and 12,000 ft., stopping at Rochester en route. I suppose it was about 400 miles. There is more agriculture in these parts and you notice the contour plowing which was originally introduced by Jefferson.

We caught a hasty glimpse from our taxi of the statue of President McKinley (who was murdered here) and now we are off to a luncheon and afternoon lecture.

6.20 P.M. Well, we have been to Canada! (We globe-trotters take nations in our stride.)

The lecture to the Garret Club was successful—it is a club founded 60 years ago by the ladies of Buffalo who had got tired of being excluded from the clubs of men. Some founder members still survive and it has become grand and difficult to get into with a long period (of years) on the waiting list. I wonder how soon it will be before I get vain and do an unsuccessful talk? The ladies laughed a lot (women are not usually very fond of humor) and clapped heartily and stated they were pleased.

Afterwards Mrs. Campbell (?) very kindly drove us to the Niagara Falls. On the whole I agree with Oscar Wilde, who said that all newly wedded American ladies were taken there on their honeymoon and it proved to be the first if not the greatest disappointment of their married lives. Carol, who had wanted to see them from before leaving England, was satisfied. The great-grandfather of our hostess, a Mr. Schoellkopf, had first harnessed their power, which is moderately impressive. At the top of the Horseshoe, where the green water curves into the bank, there is a rather pleasant watery feeling which makes you half want to enter the great lively emerald current and go over the edge. About half a dozen boats a year do. They are of fishermen upstream who have lost their anchors or whose engines have failed. But there is a definite attraction, not suicidal, something like the water-chute in a swimming pool, which makes a swimmer almost want to sport with the fall. I can understand why people go over it in barrels. It is asking you to.

I was more interested by childish oddments.

I got a new stamp on my passport (Canada). I saw the swinging and bell-ringing Stop signal for railway crossings. I found that the moment I was on semi-British soil again they could grow proper grass. I found a new version of rusticated masonry. I was told that the Dutch Elm disease (which Thurber claimed his uncle died of) had started again. I realized that the vast new roads of this continent are all postwar.

The Pan-American Exhibition, at which President McKinley was murdered, had a show of *diving elks.*

The L on an elevator (lift) stands for lobby.

I must write more about the President's assassination, but at present we are going out to dinner.

18 · 10 · 63

The huge city of Buffalo is not beautiful. Its domestic architecture is still square, wooden, Canadian, almost pioneering. The first child was born here round about 1800 and her name was Winne Ransom. Now there are a million people.

The *raison d'être* of the place seems to have been the Great Lakes. The produce of the vast Middle West in grain and steel and other products found its transport down these lakes as far as Niagara, which must once have been a sort of portage, and now has locks to bypass it and connect with the St. Lawrence Waterway. I think I am beginning to get a picture of the continent, helped by seeing so much from the air.

Buffalo, like Washington, was burned by the English in the War of 1812. The Americans still feel grumpy about this.

President McKinley was a fat man. His anarchist assassin

put on an arm sling, as if he had a broken arm, and concealed the revolver inside it. He shook hands with the President with the other hand, drew him to him, and shot him point-blank twice in the stomach. Being a fat man, McKinley took about four days to die. The stomach was the worst place to shoot him in.

The geese (Canada and Snow) are at present migrating down Lake Erie, but poor T. H. White with his lectures and receptions sees nothing of this.

This morning we had a conversation about car graveyards as we drove to the airport. Where to put the used vehicles, in their millions? Carol said, "Why not throw them in the sea?" This made me think it would be good sport to send them all over Niagara Falls, and, further to that, why not send the *Queen Elizabeth* over when she is due for scrap? Unfortunately there would not be enough draft for her in the rapids above, and anyway her bows would hit the bottom long before her stern came over the top.

We flew from Buffalo to Chicago in an Electra 2 at 18,000 ft. in an hour and a half. It must have been about 475 miles at about 320 m.p.h.

At first we saw the geometrical roads of Canada and Michigan, then thousands of little lakes. Then we were flying over cloud and perhaps ground rain, which hid Detroit.

I would have liked to have seen Detroit, the birthplace of all those cars which are choking America, and Henry Ford's museum and village. It would have been nice to land and watch an assembly line and see the strange magpie collections of old Henry—the chair Lincoln was assassinated in and the first model gramophone and Wilbur Wright's bicycle shop and Edison's laboratory (with original rubbish heap) and an authentic Cotswold cottage.

We saw nothing of Chicago except the corridors of the airport along which we scampered. Carol says we get back to Chicago later in the tour, and if so we must see the Water Tower. Apparently it is an American Victorian building after my own heart. Barbara Kreutz and Ellen Fleming write that it is a "crenellated, turreted mock-castle, built of the coarse yellow stone so characteristic of nineteenth-century Chicago [and] embodies all the provincial ugliness of the town, yet it is so bad that it is endearing." This sums up my tenderness for such architecture.

I also want to see "Mrs. Thorne's Rooms." They are about 50 miniature rooms of dollhouse furniture in various period styles covering four centuries. "Meticulous copies, and there are tiny petit-point carpets and hangings made from rare old silks and brocades and exquisite miniature chandeliers and sconces."

We also might have a look at a few gangsters.

Chicago is the second biggest city in America, a quarter of its people are Negroes, it is called "the Windy City" from its intense winter cold, it has a great selection of foreign elements, it used to be very ugly, and from its famous shop of Marshall Field came the young Selfridge to England.

This is being written at 31,000 ft. and 600 miles an hour over the Rocky Mountains. We have crossed the wide Missouri! We are in an American Airways astrojet (a Boeing 990) which we entered along a covered ramp as if it were the *Queen Elizabeth.* It is provided with oxygen masks for emergency, its drinking-water system has broken down so we can't have coffee, it has four lavatories, we are as usual First Class, and our luncheon has been magnificent. Carol had Lobster Américaine. I had crêpes Florentines. We were offered, but refused, champagne. (I have kept to my water wagon religiously, to escape the fate of Dylan Thomas and Brendan Behan, for two months now.)

Above the high, sunny, flocculant clouds which hid the Rockies from us I said to Carol, "These are *American* clouds, don't forget." "Well, you never know where they've come from." "No, they are *American* clouds and they have come specially for us."

When we reach San Francisco we will have covered 2,310 miles today, will have crossed four time lines (Eastern Standard, Central Standard, Mountain Standard and Pacific Standard) and my wristwatch will be three hours wrong. They will go to bed in Buffalo three hours before we do. It makes a long day of it for us, traveling with the sun.

19 · 10 · 63

We looked down on the barren, olive-green plains and uplands of Utah, where covered wagons had labored along like tortoises, taking days where we were taking minutes (literally ten miles a minute). There were more and more mountains between the clouds. It was bumpy and we were told to fasten our seat belts. America was empty again as we descended the endless foothills. Eventually there was another of these landings over water, like Boston, and we found ourselves in a shabby San Francisco taxicab heading for this pleasant Moorish hotel with Tudor trimmings.

Last week had tired us—so much travel and outgiving—and our first impression of San Francisco was of its grubbiness. Today is the first of three days without lectures, so we will look about us and revive.

One of the wonderful things about America is that it is a pioneer country which *knows it is present at its own birth.* For instance, it is already restoring and preserving the Front Street saloon area at Dodge City in Kansas, where Wyatt Earp and Bat Masterson were so lately establishing the Pax Americana with guns. It is as if William Rufus had already begun to preserve the site of the battle of Hastings.

They may be romanticizing their history—which is always slated by the visitor in any case—but they are at least doing something about it.

This reflection has nothing to do with San Francisco (once, and in fact till the Gold Rush which began in 1847, merely the Spanish township of Yerba Buena) but is written down after breakfast while Carol struggles with her heavy duties as secretary. Without her care and kindness and efficiency this tour would not exist.

6 P.M. Well, it hasn't taken long to fall in love with San Francisco.

We had the good luck to come across a really friendly and intelligent cabdriver, Mr. George Sommer, a retired policeman who divides his time between running a taxi and commercial fishing in his own motorboat. He gave us his whole morning very cheaply, shutting off his meter whenever he could so as to improve our minds about this fine, abundant, diverse, individual city. Some of his information may have been a bit inaccurate, but we have no time to check.

The three great wonders of San Francisco are a) the roller-coaster gradients of Nob Hill, b) the Chinese quarter, and c) a magnificent stucco building (described by Mr. Sommer as being of papier-mâché, which it just might have been) called the Palace of Fine Arts.

It seems that the lower dockside areas of the port near Fisherman's Quay used to be a bit homicidal in the early days, so the richer tycoons moved their families to the comparative safety of Nob Hill—just as the King of Naples moved up from the harbor during times of crisis. Sommer said that the ridge rises to 906 ft. and can have a gradient of 25° or 30°. It is prodigious. The brakes of his taxi are reset every day and renewed every month. There is a strict traffic regulation by which parked cars must have their front wheels locked against the curb. Going down these fearsome chutes in a taxi is as breathtaking as anything at Blackpool. It feels like 45°.

In the early days there used to be horse-drawn trams for these heights, but the poor creatures were always slipping on the steep, brick-paved roads and having to be destroyed there and then because of broken legs. A lady called Mrs. Leland Stanford, to whom all horses and decent people ought to be grateful, was distressed by this and managed in 1873 to institute the cable cars which are still in use. They run on a cable like a funicular railway and can manage nine miles an hour. They are reversed at top and bottom on a turntable.

China Town must be the only China Town outside China which is not a phony for tourists. To begin with, it houses 22,000 Chinese. The streets are gay with paper lanterns and Oriental street lamps and shops selling genuine goods from across the Pacific. The basically American architecture has here taken a wonderful Chinese slant, just as New York has often taken a Babylonian one, and the result is an *individual* style of the greatest charm and interest.

I bought Carol a pair of cuff links which said LOVE in Mandarin characters, and for myself a pair which said PROSPERITY.

San Francisco has several exotic colonies, apart from the Chinese. For one thing the Beatniks began here (contemporaries of Mort Sahl) and there is a restaurant where the entertainment is by males dressed as females. Mr. Sommer said it was easy to obtain marijuana. He had himself in the course of duty shot dead an addict who had first taken two shots at him and wounded his companion. He said he only began to tremble ten minutes afterwards.

The third great wonder among so many others, the Palace of Fine Arts, was built for the 1915 Exhibition. It is a terrific, exuberant yet not incorrect Corinthian building centered around a rotunda on a lake with duck and gulls and geese on it. It is partly chocolate and partly white, a sort of very late Roman extravaganza, and it is coming to bits. It is a miracle that its stucco should have stood up to the Pacific climate for 48 years. At present it looks imperial, slightly dotty, impressively ruined, romantic and poetical—everything that the wildest Corinthian ought to be. It is imperative that it should be preserved, and Mr. Sommer said that some sort of fund for doing so had in fact been started. The "papier-mâché" is coming off the lathes, and the statues have lost their heads. It is a sort of imperial dream by Cecil B. de Mille in lath and plaster. I discovered that its actual materials were chicken wire, horsehair, gypsum and hemp.

Incidentally, there is a fine piece of American Romance architecture in the Church of St. Peter and Paul (I think that was the name) which de Mille is said to have used in *The Hunchback of Notre Dame*. Outside it there is a statue to the earthquake disaster which looks as if the Laocoön had gone mad and joined the fire brigade.

We saw what Mr. Sommer described as "Sacramento sea gulls" and also the fleet of pleasure fishermen crowded in their expensive speedboats in search of striped bass.

It was nice to see that all the cops still in the force exchanged affectionate salutations with Mr. Sommer wherever we went. He said, yes, there had been a certain amount of police corruption in the lawless days. He observed that a city gets the police force it wants.

San Francisco is obviously a most individualistic if not eccentric town which I am going to love very much, and its police seem to correspond to it.

After lunch we took a Grey Line Tour of more than three hours, to see the sequoias, etc., at the Muir Woods National Monument (Park). I reluctantly took photographs of the Golden Gate Bridge—which anybody can have, so far as I am concerned, because it leaves me cold to know that something is only the biggest or fattest or thinnest or something of its kind. Also we photographed the Bay Bridge to Oakland, which is 8½ miles long—the longest in the world.

We saw the eucalyptus trees which shed their bark as well as their leaves, but which are useless for carpentry because nails split their planks. We wound up suicidal corkscrew roads in the 12-ton bus through a landscape or bayscape which was faintly like Hong Kong's, with its flat-roofed homes (American for houses) and artistic colonies and snatches almost of Polynesia. You have to remember that San Francisco is a Pacific civilization. It can have phone boxes shaped like Chinese pagodas.

Carol went on the guided tour in the tree park, but I wandered off into the great trees alone (contrary to the notices beside the paths). The impressive thing is the stillness. Redwoods are acid or something, repulsive to insect and bird life and hence to other kinds of animals. I did not see a single squirrel or any other living thing except some small salmon parr (?) in a trickling burn among the hushed rufous massive tree trunks. I did hear one jay.

I used to know a Wellingtonia at Stowe whose blotting-papery bark belied its seeming cragginess by tolerating quite a hard thump with the fist, without hurting. The two trees I thumped at Muir Woods seemed less well cushioned.

The bus came back over the Golden Gate Bridge—very close to which a courageous young woman whose name I have forgotten recently fought a shark to save a man, who subsequently died in the hospital.

We entered the city by a different route, along the wide pink boulevard called Venice Avenue. This part is exactly as old as I am. It was all destroyed by the earthquake in 1906 which led to 3 days of fire and 700 deaths and the Laocoön monument which we photographed.

It was a grayish, sunless day and my many photographs of fascinating architectural fantasies may not be very good.

After dinner in the evening we took a taxi down Chinatown, to photograph the signs lit up in Chinese. Unfortunately they had not switched on the paper lanterns. We went on as far as the Palace of Arts, which was said to be illuminated, but it was not. I fear that San Francisco, like most individualists, is inclined to be irregular. I did get a long-wanted picture of steam coming out of the street, but I think I may have miscalculated the flash.

Everybody in San Francisco seems to go to bed early or stay up all night.

Fig leaves and statues of firemen, Confederate generals, etc. It is literally true that in all of America which we have seen so far we have not come across a single entire nude male in a public place. I passed last winter in Italy and made a vague study of fig leaves. In Florence, statues can afford to go without them—much to their advantage. In Rome, presumably as a gesture toward the Catholic dogmas, they wear small maple leaves. In fiery Naples, for fear of inflaming the passions, they wear rather large scrolls, like sporrans. In America no form of leaf is sufficient. A swirl of stone drapery has to be wafted across the loins. Does this mean that Americans are even more virile than Neapolitans? Or has the censorship of females extended so far as emasculation? (In San Francisco I should have thought not.) The typical American statue wears a heavy frock coat and carries a saber, a ramrod or a fire hose, to symbolize his genitals.

20 · 10 · 63

They played "Hearts of Oak" on TV yesterday for a football match. I mildly remarked on this to a sailor who was sitting at our table, only to discover, to my horror, that for him the tune was his national anthem—"The Star-Spangled Banner!" He forgave me.

The four great tycoons of San Francisco while the gold rush was making it a great city were Collis Huntington, Leland Stanford, Mark Hopkins and Charles Crocker. When they came to power, the waterfront had been called the Barbary Coast. You got shanghaied there. I suppose it must have been "robber barons" like these who struggled for control of the transcontinental railway, and Wells Fargo (whose banks are still all about here) and the rest of the economy now romanticized in "Western" movies. The grandeur of their taste in domestic architecture is still displayed in the lobby of the Fairmount Hotel.

The cooking here is excellent, even in self-service diners which are quite cheap comparatively with the rest of the U. S. Self-service seems to be a feature of the West and drugstores tend to be what they call themselves, i.e. pharmacists rather than eateries. Food specialties are Chinese dishes, abalone, sand dabs, Rex sole, Dungeness crabs and Olympia oysters. Last night I had a delicious pepper steak and we both had waffles with maple syrup for breakfast this morning.

I am beginning to call lifts "elevators," America the "United States," films "movies," tonic water "Quinine," and coffee "cawfee"—otherwise I wouldn't get what I wanted. My Cambridge accent is as fascinating to them as theirs is to me. We can count on half the fingers of one hand the people we have found unpleasant, from here to New York and everywhere else.

San Francisco *is* a bit grubby—its taxis old—and all the better for that. The lift in our hotel (sorry, elevator) has a temperament of its own and does not have a marker to tell you what floor you are at. It takes you up or down accordingly as somebody outside may have pushed a button since you did, and you have to peer anxiously out of the door for a room number to determine which floor you have reached. The proprietors and other guests are friendly and helpful and discuss their possible destinations in the elevator, for which we all feel affection.

The shops are magnificent, and their Chinese goods (got from Japan because of Communism in China) are well above the tourist level.

I would like some vice, but Carol threatens to come too.

Day before yesterday we must have flown near Lake Tahoe and the ghost towns of the forty-niners on their gold rush. Imagine the tribulations of the original covered-wagoners who once plodded the Sierras thirty thousand feet below our whistling wings—the snows, the waterless deserts of Nevada and Utah, the immense Rockies, the enemy Indians of the Great Plains. Above all, imagine their *distances*. It took four months to come from Missouri to California. At the Donner pass a party under the leadership of a man called Donner got badly organized and caught in the snow. "After terrible privations they descended to cannibalism and murder." We were eating *homard américain* above their glaring phantoms.

Today we had a busy morning establishing contact with our sponsor who, unlike our previous academic or social patrons, is in the business for profit. "Town Hall Forum of the West" was founded by him 27 years ago as a money-making venture, at a time when he had eleven dollars in his pocket. It has been addressed in the Curran Theatre by everybody from H. G. Wells to Bertrand Russell. So, as it was a commercial matter of advertisement, I had to be interviewed and photographed by the *Examiner* (a Hearst paper?) and by the S. F. *Chronicle*. Tomorrow I shall have to be interviewed on the radio. He gave us a snack at the Sheraton Palace, an American-Ionic-Beardsley piece of opulence which was built in 1902 and withstood the earthquake. He (Dr. Rappaport) observed in his Russian (?) accent that America was like a young man who has not yet had enough experience of life. I asked how young? He said, "In his early thirties."

We escaped by about three o'clock and took a boat trip of an hour round the bay. Alcatraz, we learned, was once an island covered with pelicans, and the prominent Coit Tower—a memorial to the great fire—is built on purpose in the shape of the nozzle of a fire hose.

Afterwards we went shopping in the tourist shops of Fisherman's Wharf and bought ourselves spiky balloon fish and apaché tears (a semiprecious stone) and Siamese cuff links (for Carol) and abalone cuff links for me.

We had an early dinner in a seafood restaurant for trippers, and deservedly paid too much for a perfectly horrible meal of abalone, which tasted of fishy veal ill-fried long ago in mineral oil. Fisherman's Wharf has been so commercialized that I doubt if you would meet a real San Franciscan in it, and it can only be visited as a joke.

21 · 10 · 63

Today has been a day of some confusion.

Thanks to my lecture agents, who forgot to get me a work permit, we spent the morning trailing along consular corridors trying to transform my B-2 visa into an H-1, which permits me to gain money lecturing. Hitherto I have been working illegally.

This wasted most of the morning, which might have been devoted to rest or to San Francisco, but we did have time for a good shopping tour and lunch in Chinatown. We bought several wonderful cuff links.

Our Russian-born sponsor here is a character out of Chekhov. He understands little of what either of us says, listens to less, and is disordered as to appointments, times, places and other business details. He has introduced me in his brochure as "Terrace" Hanbury White and the mysterious sentence with which it concludes has neither verb nor predicate.

So far as Carol could understand him, he had arranged to meet us at the K.C.B.S. radio station in the Sheraton Palace between 1:30 and 2 P.M. I went there by myself at about 1:35, found a vacant elevator, rose in it, and walked straight into the studio where the broadcast had already begun. Fortunately for all concerned I am a seasoned ham on radio as well as TV, so we went straight on from there—the broadcast interview, commercials, question time, etc.—lasting till 2 P.M. Mr. Rappaport never did turn up.

I found a telephone message from him at the hotel, countermanding previous arrangements, when I got back. It is to be hoped that the lecture itself will take place at the stated time and place tomorrow, but whether Mr. Rappaport takes the same time and place seems open to question.

It is fair to add that he understands as little of Carol's and my English as we do of his nine languages. He is not a born American and has had a varied career. He was born in Russia and saw his father and brother shot before his face. He became an opera singer, but only after studying medicine. He lost all his money. He returned to medicine. He became a Jewish pastor or cantor as a side issue. He started this Town Hall Forum thing 27 years ago on 11 dollars. He claims to speak the nine languages, but listens to or understands few of them. (My own communications with him are safest in Italian.) He is a kind and friendly person, closely resembling the White Rabbit in *Alice.* (He left all his papers at the newspaper office yesterday and may still be rushing up and down elevators in search of them.) We had said it very loud and clear, we had gone and shouted in his ear—that we would be out during the morning in pursuit of visas—but it made no difference.

Our Chinese lunch again ended with pastries that contained printed prophesies. Carol's said, *You will be fortunate in everything you put your hands to.* Mine said, *This is the month that indicates your greatest success.*

One of the papers has misrepresented me as saying that San Francisco is in American Gothic, which of course it is not. The Gothic went with the earthquake. I was talking about other cities.

A characteristic sound of S. F. is the rattle of the cables inside their steel sheaths below street level as they pull up the "trams."

The taste shown by the more expensive furniture shops, picture shops and art shops is sumptuous, a magnificently high standard.

During the broadcast I had to answer questions put to me over the telephone by listeners. I thought this an excellent variant from the English method.

The taxi drivers of S. F. are charming and friendly, and on the whole I believe this is the *happiest* city we have visited.

Carol has gone off to have dinner with a friend who lives here, so now is my chance to go out on the town.

22 · 10 · 63

We saw a couple of Brewer's blackbirds at Fisherman's Wharf, the day we took the trip around the Bay. Some expert had informed Carol that these were American robins! I don't have enough time for birds or trees, or people for that matter.

This was partly remedied last night. I was speeding out hot-foot for a bit of night life when I found a couple waiting for me in the lobby, who had been there for two hours unannounced. They were Dr. and Mrs. Bill Walsh, whose efforts to educate themselves and twelve children (the thirteenth died at birth) had once been celebrated by a six-page story in *Life* Magazine. So we went out to dinner together at the Sir Francis Drake, a Dutch treat. They told me the fascinating story of their lives—cultured Roman Catholics of great charm who had been responsible for their own "population explosion," which I envied. They gave me a photograph of the family, one nineteen-year-old already missing through marriage.

The lecture this morning was a bit of a chaos, but passed off pretty well. For one thing Dr. Rappaport had absent-mindedly invited two separate people to introduce me—it was with difficulty that I retrieved one of them from the wings—a Professor Churchill who was being ignored in the general confusion.

The lecture was in a commercial theatre, the Curran, where I held the stage alone, following *The Time of the Barracudas, How to Succeed in Business Without Really Trying,* and *Carousel.* Among a vast list of lecturing predecessors were Winston Churchill, Mrs. Theodore Roosevelt, Mr. Nehru and Sir Edmund Hillary.

The lights failed twice, the lead of my neck microphone was trapped in the wings, where Dr. Rappaport had been winding himself up in it, and the first introducer forgot to introduce the second one. I did not win as many laughs as I would have done from a less middle-aged audience (who had paid for their seats, about $7) but I did win a reasonable proportion and nobody coughed or went out and they did applaud at the end. It was a bit like a charity matinee or benefit performance, such as is disliked by most actors, and, considering the circumstances, it left me still as fond as ever of S. F. A paying audience, unlike an academic one, is inclined to be not quite on your side. They are inclined to sit back and say, Very well, now show us what you can do.

After only a couple of days you begin writing S. F. affectionately, instead of San Francisco.

I signed about sixty novels and after the lecture we had a polyglot dinner with Dr. Rappaport at the Clift. He now wants to fly to Mexico and book Richard Burton.

This is the end of our too-short glimpse of San Francisco, which we left with an eyeful of Benjamin Dufano's strange, interesting and phallic statue of the Madonna at the airport. There is at least one other by him, of St. Francis, in the city. They are *controversial,* explained our friendly cabdriver.

Our United aircraft to Los Angeles was a 720 jet which had been suffering from trouble with its pressurization. The result was that we started late, just in the afterglow of sunset. The night flight over the jeweled town was stunningly beautiful—the amazing richness of the street signs from the 29,000 feet which we eventually reached, their rubies and emeralds and diamonds scattered below us and the *procession* of jewels along the roads, for the cars with their headlights were following each other bumper-to-tail, with the result that you got a string of diamonds *which steadily moved* as if you were running an endless string of them through your hands! Not only jewels, but moving ones! We soared up high, as these jets so quickly do, above the clouds into a sunset like a war medal ribbon, and there was the new moon in silver above the jewel box.

Flying into the outskirting townships of Our Lady the Queen of the Angels of Porciuncula (Los Angeles) I noticed that this profusion of colored brilliants was not really a jewel box or a scattering of gems like the colorless lights of London. The little towns were more like tangled necklaces thrown down along the highways, and the advertisements for Dunked Donuts which might have seemed garish from close to were the most rich, the most glowing, the most Aladdin-like treasuries of precious stones. In England, where a night flight is also beautiful, they would have only been diamonds. Here they were bloodstones, topaz, sapphires, twinkling on the velvet of the night.

All I know about Los Angeles so far is that it covers 450 square miles, an endless flat industrial city which is still, as San Francisco was in the middle of the last century, more or less being pioneered. Hollywood, which was responsible for the start of its gold rush, is over. Other industries, of oil (gas) or airplane construction or rocket making, etc., have taken the impetus and with 7,000,000 inhabitants already it still has 30 people every hour coming here to live. Yes, said our cabdriver, but how many are going away every hour?

(This cabdriver had been held up and robbed by colored passengers four separate times. It makes me scared, he said apologetically, do you think I ought not to be? No, we both said, anybody would be scared after four times.)

Three million four hundred thousand automobiles pass daily along the roads of Los Angeles.

We have covered about 370 miles today.

Carol and I are developing a new form of life, not hitherto known to anthropologists. It has unusual features. Part of the time we are *giving out* like dynamos, part of the time we are *taking in* like vacuum cleaners, and the only time we can pause for rest is when there is no possibility of either, i.e. at airports. Most people must think of airports as busy places. To us they are havens of rest, and we enjoy waiting for connections. You are enclosed at an airport. You can't see anything of the city you are in, neither to give to it nor to take from it. We have also become addicted to airplanes—peaceful places from which you can serenely observe the passing continent. I expect that in time we shall grow some physical peculiarity like gills or lungs or fins, suitable to our strange environment of travel, take and give.

Some organ in the brain like a concertina would be useful, with stops for inhaling and exhaling charm.

The great jets crowd round the mother airport like suckling piglets.

23 · 10 · 63

The sun rises on L. A. and there, outside the windows of our very luxurious motel—which has a coffee-making machine in each bedroom—are the palm trees of the subtropics, looking like a lot of untidy mops standing upside down. Also, very typical of every part of America, there is a garage ornamented with hundreds of small triangular pennants.

10 P.M. If I don't get this written now, the diary will fall behind and never never catch up with itself in the killing weeks that are to come.

This is a brief picture of our day. We got up at 8 A.M. I was interviewed at 9 A.M. by a newspaper. At 9:30 I recorded a broadcast by telephone, a broadcast I never did get around to hearing and so far as I know nor did anybody else. At 10 we took a taxi with a colored driver who drove us the long distance to Watts Towers. At 12:30 we lunched at a diner on the way back. At 1:30 we were picked up by Professor Arnold and motored to the University buildings where I lectured to a smallish and slightly sticky audience at 1:30. (University of S. California. N. B. This Pleasures of Learning lecture is getting stale. I must develop it and not complain about sticky audiences.) At 3 o'clock Professor Arnold—a most charming, interesting and obliging gentleman—drove us up to his rich home in the Beverly Hills, where we met his clever ex-actress wife, had a cup of coffee and were taken on a tour through those heights and back through Hollywood. At 7 P.M. (somehow I seem to have changed into a tuxedo en route) we dined with the Friends of the Library, about 70, and after dinner I spoke to them till 9:30. This talk was extempore and was a success. Now I am back in the motel, tired and writing this.

1) We had a long conversation with the Negro cabdriver. His most interesting contribution to the integration argument was this. It is useless, said he, to put white and colored children together at high school level. It must be done long before the age of puberty, at kindergarten level in fact, so that they may grow up getting used to each other. He himself (one of a family of 10) was interested in music, had broken off his formal education halfway through high school and joined the Army to serve abroad. He was willing to be friendly and ended by trusting us. He said to me very simply

when we parted, God bless you. I said, Thank you. We passed a Negro high school on our way, which seemed clean, spacious and full of happy children in the big playing fields. There was one white boy among them.

2) Watts Tower is an extraordinary fantasy built single-handed by an eccentric tile setter called Simon Rodia, by birth an Italian. It is reminiscent of the architecture of Gaudi in Spain. It is made of steel rods, mesh, mortar, broken tiles, cups, dishes, bottles, seashells, bed frames and the reversed prints in concrete of tools, hands, corncobs, baskets and the implements of a tile setter. He took 33 years to erect its astonishing spires, with no architect, engineer *or even scaffolding*. The towers are about 100 ft. high and all he had to get up them was themselves as they grew and a window washer's belt and bucket. He was forty years old when he started. When he had finished, he simply went away, nobody knows why. I believe he is still living. Asked in 1959 why he would not even talk about the Tower, he replied, "If your mother dies and you have loved her very much, maybe you don't speak of her."

I no have anybody help me out.
I was a poor man.
Had to do a little at a time.
Nobody helped me.
I think if I hire a man
he don't know what to do.
A million times
I don't know what to do myself.
I never had a single helper.
Some of the people say
what was he doing . . . some of the people
think I was crazy

and some people said
I was going to do something.
I wanted to do something
in the United States
because I was raised here you understand?
I wanted to do something for the United States
because there are nice people
in this country.

SIMON RODIA

Bureaucratic efforts have been made to tear down this strange spout of American genius, as being unsafe, but I am glad to say they have been thwarted. It was finished in 1954. It stands in the Negro quarter.

3) How can I write about Los Angeles when I have been giving out or taking in all day? It is a vast city, the largest in America for area, which has grown outwards instead of up. The poorer quarters lie forever and forever athwart its endless and rather featureless plain—7,000,000 people of which the driver claimed that 3,000,000 were colored—adorned with all the advertisements in the world. The rich, and there are thousands and thousands of them, have withdrawn to Beverly Hills above its fringes and live there sumptuously in rather Chinese-looking cliff dwellings. They think nothing of bulldozing a mountain or two to landscape a garden, drive or garage. Our hosts the Arnolds had pictures on their walls which would not have been out of place at the Tatti or the Pietra. In fact the whole expensive suburb reminds you of the environs of Florence and Fiesole.

Los Angeles is suffering the transition that happened to Buffalo and that seems usual in American cities. They grow outwards from the center, which decays into a slum, and finally the tycoons of the periphery repurchase the middle bit and erect their civic center on it with great magnificence.

This re-erection has not yet been completed in L. A., with the result that the poor man's plain is still unprepossessing and apparently interminable.

We drove past the mementos of Hollywood's greatness, the footprints in concrete, the film stars' portraits set in the pavements, the crazy cinema called Grauman's Chinese Theatre—all of them matters which will one day be touchingly romantic with a different romance from the one they started with.

Professor Arnold said that the rebuilding of a civic center followed a 45-year cycle.

At present there is just this enormous subtopia traversed by a couple of glittering boulevards and a few noble avenues of gigantic palm trees, the whole being distantly bounded by a landscape of hills a little like Hong Kong's.

How inadequate is this description of a living day! But I am too tired. We will be coming back.

Spanish and Mexican influences here rightly touch the American stream.

24 · 10 · 63

We are to fly this morning 242 miles over the Mojave desert to Las Vegas, where they gamble. Perhaps this is the most tantalizing part of our tour—going so near to so much we ought to see and probably not seeing it.

It seems that the three fabulous cities of bare Nevada were

Virginia City, now mostly decayed, and Reno where you go to be divorced, and this Las Vegas, a city of the night.

The Comstock Lode of gold took 30,000 people to Virginia City in the 1870's, the richest strike in history. It produced 400 million dollars in twenty years. Here, about 400 miles to the north of where we fly—a short distance in our itinerary—were the villainous mine owners of the Western movies who built great palaces "fitted with marble and gold, dressed their wives in Paris velvets and imported entire opera companies for one evening's entertainment." Now only the old Opera House remains.

The state of Nevada lives off her gambling reserves and it is to the freakish gambling town we are going, but we shall miss a close view of the eternal descent—we fly over Death Valley, I think—and, unless our sponsor takes pity on us, we won't see the Colorado River (30 miles away) or its Hoover Dam or the Grand Canyon in Arizona. What a misery!

I think there was a very little earthquake this morning at about 7:45. Anyway, both our beds shook gently for a few seconds, as if we were pancakes on a frying pan and the cook didn't want us to stick to it.

Note that these "villainous" tycoons *did* import opera companies. This is the whole point about America so far as we have seen it. Even the villains are idealists, willing to pour out treasure on the arts, exactly like the Medici. We are living at this very moment in a Renaissance, and so I told the Friends of the Library last night. Our millionaires are not

Borgias. Like the glorious Grand Dukes of Florence, they lavish their fortunes on beauty as they see it. This is a *wonderful* fact, perhaps the most beautiful one in the U. S. I don't mind if the beauty is a bit cockeyed sometimes, like the Grauman Theatre or even the wildest excesses of de Mille. The point is that the money *is* being spent on culture of some sort, that it is an individual culture, and that even millionaires care about it. Rockefeller and Mellon might just as well be Cosimo and Lorenzo. My greatest sorrow in these parts is that it won't be possible to visit Hearst's terrific palace at San Simeon (too far, and poor communications and no time). Grand Dukes *ought* to live in palaces and import opera companies.

25 · 10 · 63

Well, here is a date missing through pure exhaustion. I think we tore the guts out of Las Vegas—but at what cost to ourselves! At half past one in the morning I was watching Carol's tired face in the night club and wondering whether I had a right not to take her firmly home to bed. How I must recapitulate.

From 29,000 ft. in our T.W.A. Convair we peered down on the great Mojave desert, a nightmare out of Lawrence of Arabia, and wondered how the original pioneers had ever been able to penetrate it. (L. A. to Las Vegas, 242 miles.) I wish I knew what percentage did *not* penetrate it, but died of dehydration on the way.

We left the hazy mozaic tessera of Los Angeles, like a vast geometrical pavement in a Roman villa, and soared up over the mountains with their wriggly roads of dust color and sometimes the paths running along the backbone crests of ridges. How terrible to have been confronted with this additional barrier after traversing the hell of sand which we approached! Why go to the moon? For half an hour, at our great airplane speed, it was an endless dried ocean bed whose colors varied from gray to Naples yellow—not flat, but seared and gulleyed like a seaside beach whose trickles had dried. Here and there a lonely field-farm won from the chaos—miles apart—and here and there were the thin threads of roads. Carol had once driven for an hour through a sandstorm in these parts, human life lost, and the sand particles rasping the paint off the car till it might have become as clean as a whistle, as clean as the skeleton of a camel in the cruel waste. How many of those forty-niners, with Indians to massacre them (themselves living on what?) as well as thirst and hunger and desert and sierra never did arrive? Cannibalism seems almost necessary.

We landed in the clear bright waste air and knew at once why people came to Las Vegas.

The assistant dean met us, Professor McLaughlin, and after dropping our bags at the Thunderbird Motel where we were to stay, obligingly drove us to the Hoover Dam—thirty miles, a mere nothing in this continent—with our elbows out of the car windows in the heavenly sun. (He said it can be 115° in the summer, so that you can't touch the metal of the car and are miserable in any car which is not air-conditioned.) We drove and drove on a splendid postwar road through the valley soil, which is a sort of cement and won't grow anything but sage and mesquite and cactus, while round the bowl of the valley—a fit one for Childe Roland and his dark tower (probably a nuclear power station by now)—nothing lived on the sierras except a few deer and wild sheep and long-eared foxes and miniature mice and reptiles. We came to the cobalt water of Lake Mead and at last to the tremendous dam, undoubtedly one of the wonders of the world. Yet it took less than six years to make. We went across it into Arizona and composed photographs and drove the long way back to a coffee reception at the college. Enough people have described the dam, so I will skip it. Seven hundred and twenty-seven feet high, it makes Niagara look pretty silly.

The enchanting thing about the University of Las Vegas is that it is still a baby one, only six years old, with less than 1,600 students. I longed to be a godfather to it, and perhaps will be in a small way, and admired the enthusiasm of its faculty and told the meeting in the evening that I would come back in five years at my own expense and find there 16,000.

We had a little time after the reception to change and eat at the Thunderbird and lose one ritual dollar each to a one-armed bandit. Incidentally, these are the first silver dollars we have seen in the U. S. Las Vegas has to use them by the million for its slot machines. In one of the countless gambling houses—no hotel can survive unless it is a gambling house and perhaps floor show or theatre as well—in our Thunderbird they were playing *Flower Drum Song* at its theatre, a shortened version, and half the cast was losing back its pay packet at the machines—in one of the gambling houses, there is said to be a jackpot every thirteen seconds! It is fantastic to view the rows and rows of what the English call Fruit Machines, the solemn silly respectable faces of the rows and rows of trippers who worship at them, and the croupiers at the little green tables in their dozens, hobnobbing sometimes with a single customer.

The rooms are policed by visibly armed guards and the food and everything else is excellent and abundant. Since the economy of the town is based on the fruit machine and each hotel is competing with the one next door to get you to use its own machines, most of the entertainment is practically free. A non-gambler could have something like a New York holiday here more cheaply than anywhere else in the U. S.

A feature of Las Vegas hotels is that there are no windows or clocks. Gamblers must not be reminded to go to bed.

The lecture was pleasantly successful.

Afterwards, because it was our duty as reporters of the American scene, but also because the inhabitants were enthusiastic and very charming people, we went on the town with Dr. Crawford and a party. We were introduced to Mrs. Houssels, whose husband is one of the proprietors of the Tropicana, and there, till 2 A.M., we watched as her guest the *Folies Bergère!* Nothing, in my opinion, could have been more innocent and correct than this procession of very beautiful bare-breasted girls and certainly nothing could have been more professional than the tempo, the military precision of gaiety and glamour and speed, with which they displayed their touching charms. Mrs. Houssels told me that one of the girls had been given away in marriage this week by Mr. Houssels—the 42nd in four years!

The theatre only holds 400 and the cover charge for a spectacle more lavish than anything in Paris is only $5 (two or three shows a day) and the entertainers other than nubile are of the first rank. George Matson was a brilliant mimic, the acrobats who could stand on one finger were unbelievable, Silvan produced his white doves out of capsules with bewildering legerdemain, and the ballets were wonderfully lit and danced—particularly a skit on the films of the 1920's—for which the houselights were made to flicker—and a lovely cage scene in which the feline girls were the great cats.

What razzmatazz, and how immense is the innocence of America!

In some parts of Nevada prostitution is legal and controlled, as it ought to be, but not in Las Vegas, where the apparent prostitutes seem affluent, classy and on their own.

Dr. Crawford also took us to the less expensive gambling avenue (Frémont?) which caters for a poorer class of tourist and is known as Glitter Gulch. Its electric signs made it as bright as day, all lit by that Hoover Dam (as Los Angeles is watered).

Have I written before that it is ridiculous to sneer at the lighted advertisements of the U. S.? Romantic historians are always saying how wonderful Elizabethan London must have been "with all those painted inn signs swinging in the wind." Well, here you have it still alive. Why sneer? It is living, it is folk art, it is exquisite from an aircraft and I personally *like* to be saluted by an electric cowboy a hundred feet high who waves his arm in a gesture of Hi!

We tumbled blinking into bed after 2 A.M. and had to be up again at 7 A.M. to catch our Convair (another 242 miles over the eternal desert) and as we passed through the lobby of the Thunderbird the mesmerized gamblers were still at it!

We decided that Las Vegas would be a splendid place to

live, that its baby university was among the most lovable we had visited, and that when you can drive out from the *Folies Bergère* into a sunrise of the limpid desert air and be killed by a sidewinder you are certainly living your life.

26 · 10 · 63

I am still a day behind with the journal.

I wrote enthusiastically about Las Vegas, but something sad happened there. While we humans were driving downtown in all that blaze of light on pleasure bent our car drew up beside a mammoth lorry full of sheep "Going to the slaughter house" said somebody. I looked into their quiet, dignified, mountain eyes, perhaps free that very morning on the sierras between which we drove, and half the evening was poisoned for me. It was an effort to be gay.

I was a vegetarian once, for about two years, but gradually gave it up because I was such a curse to my hosts when I went out. Well, at least I can give up buying fish or meat for myself. I will eat it when provided by others, to be polite, but from the day before yesterday I have bought my last murdered animal. I have sent my last aristocrat to the guillotine.

Mrs. Coke and Mrs. Altman met us at the Los Angeles airport again, where, introduced by Dr. Dick, I was to lecture to U.C.L.A.

Carol has taken a couple of nights off to stay with friends, leaving me a mass of instructions about how to meet her at a place called Orange. I shall miss her very much, as she is already half the act.

Mrs. Coke and Mrs. Altman kindly drove me all the way to Marineland, since we had a few hours to ourselves before the evening's dinner and lecture. We had lunch on the way at an excellent Mexican restaurant whose central feature was a little garden full of well-kept flamingos, toucans, etc. What a silly zee-zee voice a flamingo has when it is scolding its mate.

It was a day of smog, and the long drive and the lack of sleep and the weeks of travel combined to make my eyes smart and I began to feel very tired.

The seals and porpoises at Marineland obviously enjoyed the tricks they played with their trainers, for reward, and somehow it was not ignoble to watch porpoises playing baseball, even if it was for bits of fish. The tanks were very large and clean, the animals were plainly happy.

Dr. Richard Freeman of London University, himself a vivisectionist when necessary, told me before I came that the antivivisection laws in England were ludicrous, but they were worse or nonexistent in the U. S. He said that behind the façade of playful mammals in some of these places there were highly intelligent creatures having electrodes thrust into their brains. How I loathe and despise the name of Pavlov and the thought of any person who can hurt these lovely beasts.

The voice of a porpoise, in air, is birdlike and twittering, a bit like a jay perhaps but much more varied and musical. Perhaps the most remarkable trick was the porpoise who willingly came out of the water to lie on dry land, to be fed and petted.

We watched live whales in the great submarine tanks, from

windows in the sides, and longed and longed to spend days there—but there was hardly an hour. What I really wanted was to get into the water with them.

Dinner was with Dr. Dick and a party at the Kirkaby Center, a central skyscraper which alters your ideas of Los Angeles and makes the panorama of plain surrounded by mountain seem beautiful.

Somebody mentioned at dinner that the last breakfast of Leland Stanford had been preserved (a wax model) at Stanford University, which was endowed in his honor. I hope so.

I was feeling like *death* when it came to lecture time at 8 P.M. Fortunately the packed audience was an adorable one, my best since Boston, and their kindness and willing laughter lifted me back to a plane of happiness and success.

Home to the same motel, to tumble into bed by 11 P.M. They had kept me at questions and signing books for an hour after the talk.

We came across several traffic cops that day (minimum fine 12 dollars on the spot) and in fact thought we had been signaled by one. Lawlessness seems to be high everywhere. At Las Vegas a lady professor asked not to be left at night till she had entered and started her car; at U.S.C. the library shuts at 10 P.M. rather than retain extra policemen after that hour to protect its virgins on the campus; there are murders in every paper, and Mrs. Coke said she would never stop for hitchhikers.

I suppose, if you are living in a Renaissance, you do have violence. We are in something like a modern Elizabethan England, and there may even be somewhere a Shakespeare now alive.

Americans and spikes. There is a spiked bar on springs which can be fitted in a road so that you can drive your car over it in one direction but not in the other. This is useful on parking lots. In a way it is like a "cattle gate" in England.

The main feature of Los Angeles is its flat vastitude and the difficulty of coping with the titanic motor freeways on which its transport depends. Once you are on a freeway you have got to look sharp, and are preyed on by traffic cops for driving too slow or for interfering with the stream of traffic. It is the least free place on earth and it is almost impossible to get on or off it at the right place.

Today, the 26th, the Cokes were good enough to drive me to Disneyland, which I felt it was my duty to visit—Mr. Disney having paid me the princely sum of 750 pounds for the rights in a film on which he is reputed to have spent five million dollars. He made the purchase a generation ago, when I was poor and innocent, and has held them strangled for more than 25 years, neither making the film nor selling them back to me, although I had other and magnificent offers.

I tried consciously to like Disneyland, and I succeeded.

The trip to the moon was splendid and the voyage in the submarine was fancifully spectacular.

We reflected as we sat in one of the cafés, among the 16,000 people who visit it every day, that all this had sprung from the brain and drive of a single individual. The enormity of Disney's fantasy, *which he has realized,* must, cannot but, compel respect. The whole tone is individual, unmistakable (you could not mistake Disneyland for anybody else's land) and a solitary homunculus has created it, with all its billions of dollars.

Yet there is something wrong with Disney.

We tried on the way home in the car to put a fair name to it. Why those awful mermaids encountered on the submarine trip? Why were they so saccharine, insipid, dishonest, unworthy, coy? Why was the sea serpent a babyhood dream, not grand or terrible or beautiful or even reptilian? Why was everything just wrong, the galleon unsailable, the whale provided with toy teeth? Why was everything a toy, in fact? Why was everything a *pet?* It seems that to Disney women, animals, children, knights, dragons and elephants are all pets. Even the mermaids were pet mermaids, dolls to play with.

Disney's is a world of dolls and dollhouses.

Chaucer believed that animals must be true to themselves. He praised a horse for being "right horsely." Disney's horses are not, his mermaids are not mermaidly nor his sea serpents serpentine—nor are his humans human. For one thing, they are all completely sexless—which, so far as I can see, cuts out about 80 percent of human life.

While I was writing this, a crazy-looking character knocked on the door and opened it at once where it faces on the yard of the motel—fortunately it was on the chain. I said, "What do you want?" "I want to borrow a quarter to take me home." I said, "No, thanks," and shut it, and hoped he didn't have a gun. Then I rang up the office, who came and chased him away as he was knocking at the room next door. He was well dressed and looked drugged.

To get back to Disney. Why must his elephants fly? Would Chaucer have thought it elephantly? Why is everything a fairy?

Yet the trip to the moon was superb. You sit round in a circle or airplane-like seats in tiers, and watch out of the circular nose or tail of the rocket. At takeoff there is actually the noise and the vibration and the fire. (To me, after all these thousands of miles, it was perfectly natural and, if I had arrived on the moon, I would at once have delivered a lecture there.) You see the earth dwindling below, the moon growing above (all this on colored movies) and the whole thing is convincing and not coy.

I longed to have had Jimmo there when he was an enthusiastic boy, and to have taken him to Merlyn's magic shop as well—where he could have bought exploding cigarettes, etc., to his heart's content. Incidentally, Excalibur was there in a corner, stuck sideways through a stone. If you could pull it out, you were at one time allowed to write your name in a book, but the apparatus is now out of action.

And further to that, a student brought me a book to sign last night and told me, when I asked him, that his name was Arthur Pendragon. So I signed it Merlyn and shook hands and said I was glad to see him again. Somehow we did this without much of Disney's whimsy—but it was touch and go. It depends on the tone.

I forgot to say that the whale we were looking at yesterday had a skin like a beech tree or a rubber tire. In places it was scratched or nicked or practically vulcanized as if for a puncture, and you felt like cutting a heart on it with JOHN LOVES MARY. Bark.

On the way back by one of the freeways (an hour's drive, here thought of as nothing) we passed a factory of U. S. Royal Tires which had been built in the *Assyrian* style of architecture! It was in working order.

I would like to visit Alcatraz and Disneyland after dark alone, after visiting hours. I would also like to go to Mexico and to Texas (which we miss) and to swim with the whale or porpoises or seals. Surely, by some sort of skulduggery, this might one day be managed? And why aren't we going to Cape Canaveral?

11:30. The infinitely patient Cokes and Altmans came to fetch me again for dinner and took me to a place which I wouldn't otherwise have known about. It was a short completely Mexican street (Olvera Street) which is fairly well known to tourists but not spoiled. The Mexican population in Los Angeles is high. There at a restaurant called the Casa de la Golondrina we ate tortillas and guacamole (based on avocados) and chile relleno with plain enchilada. The Golondrina is in a house which once belonged to the family Pelanconi. It is a state monument, being the first brick house built in Los Angeles (1850). The food was excellent and it had a good, happy floor show, including a stout white-shouldered lady in black lace, a hefty middle-aged Carmen who sang beautifully, and a pretty young dancer in red, with her castanets. It made me want more than ever to go to Mexico. We bought a few gewgaws in the street stalls outside, which have cheap and excellent pottery, etc., if you look for it.

This is getting more and more like a guidebook.

The Altmans told me of seeing in a hotel at Las Vegas a gunman sitting on one side of the room and on the other side the man he had been hired to shoot. He was only waiting for the proper opportunity and all in the room were aware of the situation and so were both principals.

It seems that gangsters are more efficient administrators of a gambling town than politicians are—they will tolerate no dishonesty or loaded dice. The innocence of Las Vegas may be maintained by the American violence in which I am beginning to believe.

I must remember to send my privately printed verses to Doris Coke.

27 · 10 · 63

Carol is away, the problem of transport makes it impossible to visit Hearst's palace at San Simeon, and today feels like the first free day I have had on this trip—nothing to give out or take in, at least till 8 o'clock this evening. It was just as well that there was no plane to catch, as the motel office forgot to call me at 8 A.M. and I slept exhausted till 9:30. This is the second time an office has failed to call as requested, and it is not safe to trust them. In future I will set a personal alarm clock as a double check.

It is very sad not being able to do the long trip to San Simeon—it would be impossible in the time I have without hiring a helicopter. It must be the very type of New Renaissance stronghold in which the American Medici that I have been thinking about indulged their longing for beauty. Also I would have liked to have seen and thought about its architecture.

We must begin asking questions about crime and violence. For instance, the porter of this respectable motel locks himself in at midnight "because he is alone at night."

Julie rang up this afternoon from New York. I am to meet Carol at Orange this evening, where we lecture, and ring Julie up when we get back, in case it is possible to have a meal with her and Tony on Wednesday, the day they get here to make another film. We shan't get back till 10:30 or 11, which will be the small hours of the morning for them.

It has been a beautifully peaceful day—even time to read a little and nothing seen or done. Lunch by myself at the restaurant which has the flamingos, which I photographed, and a lovely lazy afternoon.

Quite a chat with Julie, clear as a bell all the way across the U. S., about the wicked pleasure of becoming the sort of ham I am becoming. She says that my standing ovation in Boston was a rarity and that she has not had a very great number herself.

The modern Medici. Robber Barons who have crossed a cruel continent to make a fortune have a right to that fortune and a right to the palaces they pioneer with it. It is much to their credit that they should also endow universities and art galleries. Unfortunately it was seldom the actual trekking forty-niners and diggers who made the fortunes. It was usually their clever parasites.

Mrs. Coke and Mrs. Altman have been infinitely kind to me, taking Carol's place as my protectors, and we have had interesting conversations on the long car drives. (These freeways are dangerous as well as confusing. The high speed you have to maintain on them can result in cumulative collisions, by which a series of cars ram each other because the front one has had an accident.) We were discussing nuns, because I have a Catholic ladies' college to address tomorrow, and they told me there are two famous nuns in one of the seminaries, one very stout, the other very bony, but both as formidable as they are beloved. "They went to Turkey in disguise" said Mrs. Altman. "What sort of disguise?" "Well, I suppose as non-nuns. There are antireligious laws in Turkey and you can't get in unless." "But this is a novelty! At wartime in England we all believe that paratroopers come disguised as nuns. Here we have nuns going disguised as paratroopers! How splendid!"

Conversation in car:

"If we do get flagged down by a traffic cop, you had better let me do the talking. I can say I am an Englishman and can't understand anything at all."

"We shall have to keep our mouths shut."

"Yes, I will say you are my Mormon wives and you are deaf and dumb."

"Wouldn't it do if you just say we are not on speaking terms?"

The characteristic gesture on freeways, along which everybody belts at 65 m.p.h., is the glance over the shoulder to see what the overtaking traffic is doing.

We discussed some of the tragedies of America, the disappearance of the buffalo, the passenger pigeons and almost the wild turkey.

28 · 10 · 63

Last night I fell in love with Chapman College at Orange. It is a small one, like Las Vegas and Elkins and perhaps you could say Williamstown, and it is not state supported. I adore young creatures (Elkins was only six and Chapman had only moved to Orange ten years ago) and feel protective about them and hopeful for their future and anxious to help. Chapman is not well off. The fees are about $1,000 a year, but the cost is about $3,000, and this has to be raised from benefactors. The faculty, as has been invariable on our tour, are dedicated people moving heaven and earth for the good of the young, and in this case the young were responsive and taking advantage of their opportunity. I found out and related during the lecture a few facts about the tycoon to whom the college owes its existence, and talked about the Medici and the American Renaissance. They were a wonderful audience and carried me along on a wave of intelligence and fun.

Afterwards the dean invited me to come back and teach—which I would gladly do almost anywhere in America, except for my duty toward Jenny and the effect it would have on my income tax. All this must be researched.

Carol is back and I am safe again.

I suppose we are seeing the best of America, the young, the enthusiastic, the idealistic, the hopeful to learn. It is a lovely tour.

Carol wanted to buy presents for her family, so we spent the morning at the famous Farmers' Market. It struck me as being a collection of not particularly cheap or remarkable shops, but the fruit stalls were good if you picked a good one. I ate figs and nuts and some of a pear which might well have been a Victorian wax one. Then I left her to go on shopping, which she looked like doing all day, and went off by myself to see if I could find Marineland again and the college of Marymount where I was to lecture in the evening.

The taxi went through Palos Verdes, most beautiful with trees unknown to me, and at Marineland I was able to see the whole program and loiter about among the other tanks. Porpoises have a pronounced smile and a whale's voice is more parrotlike than a porpoise's, less twittering.

I loitered on among the simply terrible artifacts which are on sale at the shops there, waiting for the car from Marymount which was due at six, and this was lucky. By about five thirty every single tourist had left the beautiful, functional building, and the sun had set, so I climbed up and up the sloping ramps to the top deck, where the whales were. There was only one person there, a Mr. Duke Champion, one of the divers who go down to feed the fish in the main tank and who do underwater chores. We leaned over the great mammals in the subtropical darkness and quietude, while they played ponderously or gracefully among themselves their peaceful, bedtime games.

There are three porpoises in this tank and three adolescent

whales. The eldest of the whales, he told me, has become psychotic or at any rate melancholic. He is given various drugs by psychiatrists, petted, coaxed to feed by hand, but he lies most of the time at one particular part of the tank grieving about his soul or his puberty or some other matter. (Walt Whitman was wrong about animals.) One theory is that he has been too much teased by the gay porpoises, whom he can't catch but would dearly like to, and that this has been bad for his ego. He lay there sighing occasionally through his blowhole while the bedtime porpoises played about, slapped the water with their tails and actually came to the side of the dark, lapping tank to splash us in fun.

Duke, an unmarried, sturdy Englishman with the wanderlust and the strange, diver's secret knowledge, told me that the whale tank was a little dangerous. The cuts or scratches on some of the hides are love-bites, and a porpoise has razor-sharp teeth. They can gash you in play accidentally—you don't feel it underwater any more than a nick with a razor. Some divers have been bumped about. He said that it *might* have been possible for me to get a swim with them (there was no time now) with a bit of diplomacy and with the good-will of the divers, who have to stand by. I will try hard if I ever get back to L. A.

We gossiped happily in the slapping, warm darkness while the huge creatures lazily romped and gleamed and one light burned dimly saying EXIT.

Marymount turned out to be another of these small colleges of the American Renaissance which I fell in love with on sight. It has only been at Palos Verdes for three years and hopes never to have more than a thousand students. It is sumptuously built so far—for girl students only—and the of course unpaid nuns who run it are dedicated, brilliant, happy, enchanting people. The cleanliness, the liberalism, the disciplined idealism and the sound, modern but not eccentric architecture—nuns are always superb housewives who know what they want to live in—these stole my heart, as did the audience at the lecture who were as usual far too kind to my hamming. We vowed to meet again in the shortest space of time, when the new chapel and the new dormitories and the swimming pool and all the other dreams of the future have been fulfilled. They showed me with pride and hope the plans of the architects and I promised Reverend Mother, a great lady, that I would catch a cardinal for her or at any rate a couple of robber barons. Some benefactor has got to be shanghaied into giving several million dollars to this loving enterprise.

Dr. S. H. White drove me the long freeway trek back to our motel, where I arrived at midnight, after Carol had gone to bed. I have lost my address book as a result of being on my own. Dr. White advised me to read *The American Scene* by Henry James and *The Future in America* by H. G. Wells—which I will do, but not till this tour is over, for fear of prejudice. Also *Look Homeward, Angel* by Thomas Wolfe. We had a long conversation about American wives, driving down into the jeweled city under a layer of midnight smog.

29 · 10 · 63

In 1920 a Mr. Walter Knott with his wife Condelia and their small children arrived near L. A. in a Model T Ford and rented a farm to grow berries. In 1927 they bought ten acres. Today their parking lot covers 60 acres, parks 6,000 cars and in 1962 they served 1,808,344 dinners. The place supports itself on these chicken dinners and on the revenues of its shops, which sell perfectly horrible souvenirs and bric-a-brac. There are 900 employees.

Halfway between L. A. and Las Vegas there used to be a mining town called Calico. For 15 years it had a population of 3,500, and it extracted 87,000,000 dollars' worth of silver from the desert hills. It became a ghost town when its mines shut down in 1896, and in 1951 the whole thing was bought by Mr. Knott, to re-erect as the principal attraction of his Berry Farm.

It *is* an attraction. Nearly all its sights can be seen without payment, and, beneath the commercialism and the Howdy Pardner patter, you really can sense something of the dust and the drought and the desert law of guns and the *labor* of man. It is a bit folksy, a bit sentimental and falsified, a bit too comical and chamber-of-horrors-like, but it is not a fairy township in the Disney manner equipped with flying elephants. It has excellent interiors furnished with a fairly adult sense of humor (for instance, the authentic contemporary dentist's) and good museums seriously laid out, and, as I say, nearly all of it is free.

I did not know how ponderously massive the revolver of

those days could be—the movies don't do them justice. I played a hundred-year-old music box with mechanical ballet, the equivalent for forty-niners of the juke boxes which delight our teen-agers now. I was touched by the undreamed-of fate of a broken 1750 French harpsichord, beautifully decorated, which had somehow ended up in the museum of Calico. I went to the local tent theatre and saw an excellent melodrama called *A Fortune in Flames,* at which we hissed the top-hatted villain.

The saloons are fitted out as such, with notices saying that no hard liquor will be supplied to Indians, but in fact they only supply minerals to anybody. In one of them a customer is ritually shot every half-hour with a blank cartridge.

There is a booth which imitates the Town Jail. A waxwork figure incarcerated in it is called Sad-Eyed Joe. There is some means by which a concealed actor with a Western accent can see the visitors who look in at the window, and he speaks to them individually, with considerable humor. "Hiya, Buffalo Bill" he greeted me, in allusion to my whiskers, "What ya got in that thair bag of yourn?" I was as usual carrying a B.O.A.C. bag with camera stuff in it, but it was out of sight of his window. "How on earth can you see it?" I asked, peering about. "How cain I not see it?" he replied testily, at which point we were interrupted by other customers.

It was a pity my electronic flash was out of action again. I failed to get pictures of the interiors.

Carol had again taken the day off, so I viewed these wonders alone. In the evening we had dinner with Tony and Julie, and Carol stayed the night at their hotel.

30 · 10 · 63

Today we leave the endless spread of L. A., whose seven million people have four million cars and whose adolescents can get driving licenses at sixteen. I am not sorry, in spite of the kind people who live there and like all Americans are proud of their city, to get away from the flat, garish plain where everywhere is too far from everywhere else. Its symbol is the smog which it creates for itself, a layer which hurts the eyes and lies above the plain of motor fumes that make it.

We left its oil derricks and the pumps like praying mantises and the NO SMOKING signs which you find even out of doors in areas liable to forest fires. We left its industries and Standard Oil.

From L. A. to Portland, Oregon, it was 879 miles in a 720 jet of Western Airlines at 35,000 feet. I peered before we set out into the mysterious fans of its jet engines and admired, in the first-class interior, the vase of artificial flowers which adorned it.

Will artificial flowers eventually replace real ones? They don't take time and soil to grow and can be thrown away when dusty. If the imitation becomes perfect, the laws of economy will tell in their favor. Presumably they can be scented. Imitation is the sincerest form of flattery. They would be typical of Los Angeles.

I suppose we must have flown up the San Joaquin and Sacramento valleys, leaving many miles away on our starboard wing the height of Mt. Whitney (14,496 ft.) and

Yosemite Park and Lake Tahoe and Carson City and Reno where you go to be divorced (about the same size as Las Vegas where you go to gamble) and the Crater Lake. We were following the spine of the Sierra Nevada and the Cascades, an endless corrugation of crumpled paper or cardboard, desolate, terrific, lunar, deserted. Carson "was one of the legendary figures of the West who fully deserved his fame. He began as a trapper, a mountain man, in the Rockies when trappers were the only white men there, and later he guided Frémont on two epic expeditions to find a passable trail through the Rockies and the Sierra Nevadas to California. Between adventures Kit Carson lived in Taos with his New Mexican wife. He was loved and trusted by everyone who knew him, whether Spanish-American, Anglo-American or Indian. His later military expeditions against the Navajos may appear ruthless in retrospect, but even there he was only doing what seemed right and proper at the time, and doing it as decently as possible."

I will never see a "Western" again on TV or movie without feeling differently about its Hollywood nonsense, after flying across these parched, Arabian, Persian Gulf desolations and grandeurs. It was lovely to get out of the urbanness, you can't say urbanity, of Los Angeles into the empty, forbidding sierras and the Oregon pines.

Yawn as you descend in a jet, and the massive thunder of its engines re-creates itself in your ears. At the real moment of descent it rumbles.

Portland offered us an almost English landscape.

At its airport there are "roomettes" to be hired, with bed,

shower, toilet, phone and writing desk—a splendid convenience for long-distance travelers.

From there it was 339 miles to Spokane in a DC-7 which belonged to Northwest Orient—Orient because their line goes on through Alaska (Anchorage) to Japan. Its lavatory had its name also written on the door in Japanese or Chinese characters.

(How monstrous this is, to cover 1,218 miles in a couple of pages.)

We gazed down on the strange muddly mountains of the Cascade Range, like faded plush chair-arms under the fleecy clouds, and far to the northwest of us saw the great snowy sugar loaves of Mt. Rainier (14,410 ft.) and Mt. Adams, standing through and almost indistinguishable from the cumulus clouds of our broad horizon.

We landed at Yakima (much cattle and apples) where I got out to smoke a pipe in the bright, clear, northern air. Carol claimed to prefer the Beverly Wilshire and Julie's air conditioning.

Then in the desiccated panorama there were lakes like puddles in the dry beds of prehistoric rivers (the Columbia River was once forty times its present size) and few, few cars on the endless lines of road and huge parallelograms of fields. Finally there were the scablands of eastern Washington, pockmarked like a smallpox on the earth's skin.

We touched down at last at Spokane and were unexpectedly met with welcome by Dr. Agnes Colton.

She took us to the home she shares with Dr. Frances Huston for a small reception, after which we had an early dinner and were driven to our hotel—where I, very tired, write this though I had rather go to bed.

The TV interviewed us on landing. Carol was shy but allowed herself to be coaxed.

We saw a dead porcupine on the road. The only animals I meet in America have been run over.

Miss Colton and Miss Huston, who are charmers, told us of a beautiful name we had flown over—the Horse Heaven Hills, which are heavenly for horses—and also of the Mercer girls, young ladies imported into the West to gladden the hearts of the forty-niners and who mostly became the matriarchs of the richest and most respected families.

They recommended me to read *Mormon Country* by Wallace Stegner and *The Centaur* by John Updike. They had nearly all my own books, which I happily signed, and Frances is, thank heaven, a bird watcher. We have fixed to take a naturalists' expedition on Saturday.

Also, I can never again after this trip and Las Vegas sing "Clementine" without knowing what a forty-niner was.

31 · 10 · 63

The very different temperatures here (i.e. from our eighties in L. A.) vary between 50° and 31° today.

I have been trying to formulate some rules about American architecture. a) It must not try to be English or Palladian or for that matter any other sort, of any nation, that has completed itself. I must not make copies of dead things, however beautiful. b) It must remember that it is cosmopolitan. Everybody is always saying that America is a melting pot, and so it is. The influences on American art are worldwide and her buildings have every right to be influenced by the Orient as in San Francisco or by Spain as in parts of Los Angeles or by anything else anywhere. c) But these influences must only be influences, not stereotypes to copy slavishly. It is the business of the American Hebrew architect to *go on from* the temple at Jerusalem. In this sense, the Jefferson Memorial at Washington, which develops and breaks all the Palladian rules, is probably better than Jefferson's own rotunda at the University of Virginia, which is a perfect imitation. It is more American. d) There is no reason why there shouldn't be an American Gothic, or American Classical, an American Babylonian or an American pyramid. (Why isn't there one? Is it too completed? How about a five-sided one?) e) America's own contribution to architecture, the skyscraper which derives from Sierra, seems to me to be at present in the doldrums. These glass matchboxes stood on end are losing individuality and beginning to look cheap. f) Art is *not* entirely functional. A skyscraper has got to adorn itself and this is where the future of the American building lies. Art should be partly useless. The Washington Monument is. It is a good thing that business tycoons should recognize this and spend their money on it, like the Grand Dukes of Florence.

1 · 11 · 63

The journal is getting out of hand again, through exhaustion.

Yesterday the lecture at Cheney was a success. It was in the morning. We had a sandwich meal after it and caught a

Greyhound bus to drive us 80 miles to Moscow in Idaho, where I went to a faculty party, lectured again this morning successfully, banqueted with the faculty and now, waiting for the return bus, hastily fill up this.

I think I will leave the subject of east Washington till the weekend, because we are returning there to visit the bird sanctuary, and confine myself to Idaho.

Its charms are twofold. To the east there are the mountainy forests of pine with their lakes, deer and even elk and moose—a paradise which bred two kinds of world-record trout (Kamloops and Dolly Varden) and into which you may have to penetrate by pack horse. To the west there is the fertile farmland of rich volcanic soil which grows wheat and peas and which is at present responsible for the velvet texture like shot silk or corduroy of the smooth hills—the winter wheat giving a green sheen to the mud-colored earth.

Driving through all this in a bus you get a more intimate knowledge than you do from an airplane and I made the following notes on scraps of paper.

Names. Cairo, etc. There is no reason why towns in the U. S. should have English names any more than English architecture. There are in America eight towns called Moscow.

Color in concrete. We passed an eatery built of concrete blocks which had been quietly tinted in pastel shades, which looked better than raw cement.

Horses. There are two kinds of semi-Indian horse hereabouts, the Appaloosa and the pinto. Oh yes, and a third kind called the buckskin, which has a deerlike coat.

Homes. The plain, four-square architecture of these parts near Canada is very attractive and pioneerish.

Flammable. We passed what the English call a petrol-lorry which had FLAMMABLE written on the side. This is more logical than calling it *in*flammable, which ought to mean the opposite.

Lowlands of Scotland. The plain country of Idaho reminds you of these.

Lombardy poplars. These quick-growing trees were much planted by the Mormons on their travels, and Mormons have evidently been around these parts.

Farm workers. The English eye is astonished by the very very few laborers working in the huge fields. Mechanization keeps them elsewhere, perhaps mending the machinery.

Arable. I suppose we are getting some faint idea of the vast grainlands to the east of us, in the Middle West.

Elevators. The architecture of grain elevators and silos is pleasant and impressive and economical. If you get enough gray corrugated iron, high and wide and simple but particularly high, it can look splendid. The structure must be big enough to dominate its corrugations and use them as texture. The wooden ones are also beautiful, with strange angular skylines of plain un-Disney-like turrets like sentry boxes.

Halloween. Last night was the Eve of All Souls and the boys and girls of Moscow were having their dress-up festival. At one time it was rather a saturnalia. "Trick or treat" said the youthful hold-up artists, ringing each doorbell like the

Christmas waits in England, and, in earlier days, the tricks could range from stealing your doormat or smearing your windows with paint and soap to taking a buggy to bits and reassembling it on the church roof. To escape such fates you welcomed them with a Treat—candies or cookies, etc.

Moscow has now decided to cope with the wilder elements by encouraging them. The shops of Main Street *invite* the children to paint pictures on their windows, and give a prize for the best. There they all were, rows of them, witches on broomsticks and owls on tree branches and devils in realistic flames—very well done, actually an ornamental addition to the window displays behind them. Several of these waits appeared at the screen door during our faculty party, dressed as ghosts or headless people or inhabitants of outer space or devils or just dressed to fancy. Two girls of about eleven startled me, and I them, because they had read my books.

It gets tiring to keep on saying how kind people have been to us. Moscow was no exception. Now it is 80 miles back to Cheney, but a professor is taking us—it means 160 miles to him, but he is doing it voluntarily!

Moscow was once called "Hog-Heaven," because of its pasture, but the ladies did not think it was graceful enough. The University was founded in 1889. I had about a thousand who had come to listen of their own free will.

Mr. Lauber told us as we drove to Spokane of a family called Macmillan on San Juan Island in Puget Sound. They were rich, the owners of the island and of the local mine. Their mansion is now burned down or decayed but it has their mausoleum on the grounds. On top of three steps there is a stone dining table with seven stone chairs around it. A Macmillan's body is buried in each chair. Behind each chair is a column—but one column, in memory of a girl who went wrong by family standards, is broken. The view is magnificent and all about is overgrown.

He also told us that he came of farming stock himself and had been used to plowing with horses. There are no pebbles, he said, in this soil, so, when you wanted something to chuck at the lead horse in the afternoon when they were tired, you collected a bag of apples and threw them.

One of the joys of this hard tour, though it is all a joy, is to come back from a long trip of giving-out and taking-in to the comfort of good food and a luxurious hotel, and to give a shower to my old body and a lanolin shampoo to the white hair.

2 · 11 · 63

A splendid Sunday holiday. Frances Huston came to collect me at 9 A.M.—Carol being dedicated to washing her hair—and we drove over to the Turnbull National Wildlife Refuge—where the warden and his wife and son, Mr. and Mrs. and Billy Brooks, gave us all their time till about three o'clock in the afternoon. They drove us round the refuge, which is of 17,000 acres, in the Bureau's car. Five or six thousand wildfowl spend the summer there, and, as its handbook says, "during the fall period as many as 60,000 to 70,000 ducks and geese utilize the refuge area." A list of 178 species of birds was compiled from 1937 to 1956.

It is a complex of about eleven named lakes, mostly among ponderosa pines and a few beautiful aspens. It has white-tailed deer, mule deer, muskrats, minks, beavers, coyotes, raccoons, skunks, squirrels and chipmunks—some of these new to me in the wild state.

I hope I managed to get good photographs of whitetails, chipmunks, coyotes and porcupine. Among the birds I may have had good pictures of Canada geese, trumpeter swans newly introduced, California valley quail, downy woodpecker, red-tailed hawk (what I would have called some sort of buzzard) and countless waterfowl including canvasback—impressive and new to me—slim pintail, bufflehead, golden-eye, hooded and common mergansers, pied-bill grebe. We saw some beautiful western bluebirds, russet underneath and almost kingfisher blue above. Birds like chickadees and red-breasted nuthatches and juncos were novelties.

I photographed a beaver's house and some trees they had been gnawing down.

All photographers live a life of misery, regretting the picture that got away, and I could kick myself five times round the state of Washington for missing an excellent shot at a real, live golden eagle only 100 yards away—and I had the telescopic lens! Damn and damn and damn! I just waited just one half second for just a chance of a just slightly better picture, and of course he had sloped away behind the treetops without offering it.

They told me an American nettle was more venomous than an English one—its narrow, spearlike, snaky leaves certainly look so—so I had to get out and pick a leaf to see if the

English adage still held true. (Grasp the nettle and it will not sting.) It did.

The photographs of the deer and coyotes and Canada geese were fun—you practically had to shoot from the hip. How much nicer than really shooting them! With the long-distance lens at infinity and 1/500th of a second and the appropriate aperture you had to wait at the ready and fire quick.

Coyotes, those unpronounceable creatures who get called anything from Ky-oats to Coy-oatees, have always been believed by me to be hang-dog, lean, melancholy wolf- or jackal-like animals associated with the "lone prairee." On the contrary, they are evidently alert, comical, fun-loving creatures with a sensibly wary but inquisitive interest in man. Frances said that one of them had once raced her car and, on finding he could not win the race, had turned humorously away, pretending he had not been trying.

The trumpeter swans were in a pen, having been imported from elsewhere. They are to be permanently pinioned (last joint of wing removed) so as to breed here and act as decoys for a future colony. One of the males was last in the pecking order and was being prevented by the others from feeding (probably by the other male—there were two males). He will have to be fed separately, I suppose, and perhaps become partly a pet, but it won't solve his problem in the long run. Natural selection—breeding from the stronger male—does not take account of pity. I will ask Frances tomorrow to ask Mr. Brooks *not* to pinion this one. It would at least leave him free to seek his fortune elsewhere.

Not having had any breakfast, I was ravenous by teatime and had a splendid vegetarian lunch—they had kindly remembered—with Agnes and Frances at their home. They played me two wonderful discs of music by Gesualdo (Columbia ML 5341 and ML 5234) which I must buy when I get home. In a way he is a bit like Bach. They also advised me to buy four books by Elinor Wylie (*The Venetian Glass Nephew, Jennifer Lorn, Mr. Hodge and Mr. Hazard,* and *The Orphan Angel*). They drove me back to Spokane and have offered to take us the 100 miles to Pasco tomorrow, which means 320 miles for them. We can throw away our railway tickets. We made every effort not to put this burden on them, but they seem to want it. I MUST send them my poems from Alderney, and I have invited them to stay there.

Back at the hotel, dear Carol was still slightly damp but cheerful and had attended to a lot of business and shopping—including buying me a little silver hippocampus to wear round my neck.

We have also purchased a flat polished piece of cedar upon which is written A PRESENT FROM SPOKANE, WASHINGTON. It is vividly lettered BOTTOM WHOPPER and has pictures showing the fate of Unruly Husbands, Nagging Wives and Ornery Brats. I see from the papers that ex-President Truman has just submitted—at the age of seventy-eight, is it?—to a light blow on his behind as part of his initiation into some college fraternity. He observed, "Well, that wasn't too bad." I asked at one of our universities whether these ceremonies were still practiced, and was told they were.

Today, with animals and scenery and migrating geese, seems to me to have been a satisfactory way of summing up the nature of east Washington.

Mr. Brooks offered to shoot one of the porcupines with his revolver so that I could get a closer look and picture—it was as usual in a tree, where it looked like a squirrel's dray. I did not know that they frequented trees, which they damage by barking them. But I begged him off. We threw some stones at him to make him pose better, and left him regarding us with a round, bright, reproachful eye. I hope this will not make him be fool enough to trust other humans in future.

3 · 11 · 63

Sex in America, naked statues, etc. This matter also seems to be in a state of transition. It used to be possible to buy fairly pornographic books in New York, also gramophone records, but not to send them through the U. S. mails. Now it is possible to post erotic books to a large extent (e.g., *Fanny Hill*).

The fact remains that Americans *appear* to be terrified of sex, while at the same time—as might be expected—practicing it with vigor. At one of the colleges we visited, a member of the faculty told us that 4 percent of the girls had babies out of wedlock. At another, a girl complained of backache, was taken to the campus sanitorium and there and then produced a baby. Nobody on the faculty had noticed anything amiss! Four percent is the highest figure we have heard about, but serious extramarital relations seem to be pretty usual. Virgins are said to be rare. A Harvard psychiatrist says that the rate of non-virginity in college girls has risen to 50 percent. Perhaps the repression of Puritan civilizations—and America still is Puritan—docs lead to a great amount of underground activity.

Homosexuality is as much a bugbear as Communism is, and both are subject to witch hunts.

I think that the women have imposed the apparent sexual mores. I have mentioned these subjects tentatively in most places, just as I have asked about segregation and crime, but nearly always met with a closed face.

A funny thing about American adult males, with all their subjugation to the matriarchy, is that we have noticed they do not extend the same courtesies to women that we do. Husbands are introduced before wives, often go through doorways in front of them, and do expect to be waited on at table.

Perhaps men are the weaker sex and are assuming some of the privileges of weakness.

They are noticeably tender to the tantrums of their wives, and this I like very much. One citizen, discussing the suicide of a famous author, said: "It must have been terrible for his wife—to find that she had not been able to keep him alive, with all her love." It seemed to me a penetrating and sensitive remark.

It seems that college students are more liable to get married in America than in England. We met a married girl in South Carolina, training to be a teacher, whose husband was in Seattle—training to be a teacher! I cannot believe that this was a good basis for marriage. I don't mind what happens to the husband and wife, but what about the child or children?

In any case the whole institution of marriage is nowadays an anachronism, in England as well as in America. There ought to be two marriage certificates, call them A and B, both equally legal. If you went in for Certificate A, you would be allowed to divorce by mutual consent, but you would not be allowed to have children. You would have to be soundly fined or imprisoned for having them. If you went in for Certificate B, which could follow Certificate A and be a sort of higher grade of it, you would have to be more than 25 years of age, and divorce would be forbidden for almost any cause, and you would be allowed children. (Incidentally, the population explosion will eventually force the number of children to be limited to two—or even, for a generation, to one.) The effect of this legislation would bc slightly comical. Most young men might tend toward Certificate A, and all women who had accepted that certificate would vie with one another and nag or attempt to coax their husbands for promotion to Certificate B. The husbands might tend, round about the age of thirty, to see the point of having a family and present their gratified spouses with the accolade of the higher cert. Thus all would be well, thirty being quite young enough for the serious cares of parenthood, and it would again be established, as the Prayer Book says of matrimony, that the purpose of Certificate B was for the procreation of children. *And their education.*

The day before yesterday, when we voyaged to Moscow, we were in the country where Ernest Hemingway settled down to compensate for something by killing animals, and where Ezra Pound was born. We also crossed the trail mapped out by Lewis and Clarke, the two explorers who opened up the Northwest for exploitation.

Jefferson had made the Louisiana Purchase in 1803, and in

1805 these two men came down the Snake River into the Columbia River and thence to the Pacific. They had with them an Indian squaw named Sacajawee, whose statue, with a bird in her hand, is at Cheney College. There were three tendrils of colonization stretching for California at that time—a Russian one coming down from Alaska, a Catholic missionary one coming up from Mexico, and Jefferson's little expedition cutting across the middle. Lewis and Clarke won the competition and it was somehow satisfactory to me to cross their path in these still-rural and sometimes unexploited areas.

We drove 160 miles today to Pasco over the vast, flat, yellow, sunburned, grassy plain—like an immense edition of Salisbury Plain in England.

Its sagebrush and tumbleweeds hid jackrabbits, cotton-tail rabbits, mule deer, coyotes, ground squirrels and I suppose rattlers. Over all there reigned a few Swainson's hawks. We had a very close view of one on a roadside post. But there were few of anything, and humans at about nought to the square mile. In fact, even in the nature reserve yesterday there were not many of anything to be seen, not by the standards of English nature reserves. The enormous world of the U. S. is underpopulated in all respects—by men, birds or beasts. You would never get here the sort of dawn birdsong which almost deafens you in Alderney, in the spring.

We passed a township once called Hell-to-Pay, but since renamed by a conscious pun, Eltopia.

Indians used to eat the root of the camassia lily roasted. When it was in season, the nomad tribes used to foregather at the valleys where it was obtainable and, as it were, pasture on it as geese do, i.e. without competition between groups. It was gathered by the women, who did not fight each other.

We discussed a rumor that President Harding had been murdered.

The ladies had lunch with us at Pasco, an industrial town where two railways meet at a marshaling yard, and the Columbia River also passes, and then left us for their long drive home. I settled down to fill up this, and to write to the game warden at the Turnbull Refuge about that trumpeter swan.

4 · 11 · 63

The three railways of Pasco are the Northern Pacific, the Great Northern, and the Spokane, Portland and Seattle. Also it is not one river but three—the Columbia, the Snake and the Yakima—which serve the vicinity. So it is a communications center in the flatness, patronized by General Electric, to which has now been added an atomic plant which President Kennedy dedicated last month. But our visit was a disappointment. The airline by which we had to fly out had canceled our flight for an earlier one, with the result that it was about a matter of Hail and Farewell, leaving us ignorant of far too much. The lecture was a success (this is getting monotonous and may be hubristic) and everybody was kind to us, but it was maddening to go away again so quickly. It is the largest atomic plant in the world, and we might have been shown over it.

The Columbia Basin College, which had paid the usual great sum for my speech, is only 8 years old, during which time it has grown from 295 students to 1,500. Before the lecture we all stood up and repeated the oath of loyalty, one hand across our chests. Afterwards there were a few minutes to meet the faculty over a snack meal, and then Dr. Ware and Dr. Donovan took us to the airport. Luckily the aircraft was late, so we had time for a little conversation.

The college is doing an Ibsen play next week. It is fully integrated and Dr. Ware was angry because, on a visit to the South, he had seen some colored people sit down in the middle, not the back, of a bus. "The driver did not speak to them. He picked up a wrench and went after them in silence, and they hustled to the back seats like cattle."

I noticed that we were referring to places like "Marseilles, France." For some reason this amuses English people, who think there is only one Marseilles in the world. How insular and ridiculous! In the first place, it is charming of Americans to name towns in honor of other European ones, and in the second place, when you have eight Moscows in America, it is not only reasonable but essential to talk of the prototype as "Moscow, Russia." These places have been named with love and sentiment by people who have come from the originals and wish to remember them. I would like to start a settlement and call it "Alderney, Idaho."

They saw us off from the desert airport, across which the

tumbleweed was blowing. It was a humble DC-3 with the two engines of the Dakota and it lifted us over the three towns and the three rivers for our trip of about 200 miles. I have discovered to my surprise that I adore flying again and can't stop looking out of the window and thinking about geography, now a living thing.

We flew near what was once Fort Walla-Walla, and beneath us a missionary called Marcus Whitman had been massacred with his wife Narcissa, by Indians (Cayuse), in the 1820's. We soared up the Cascade Range, Mt. Rainier cloud-hidden on our port wing. One trouble is that we were seeing things at a particular season. Perhaps the Cascades really are so when the snows are melting, but now, at the end of Indian Summer, they were a khaki dryness.

We bumped through and over the cumulonimbus, seat belts fastened most of the time. The mighty sequoias were below us, with some snow already on the fuming mountain-tops and sometimes as much motion on the aircraft as we get in *Popsy II* on the fierce seas of Alderney. Our shadow fled beside us in a rainbow halo on the icy mist.

We dropped down at last to the town-speckled woodland and the islands of Puget Sound. There were the countless private docks or piers for pleasure boats—for the people here are said to live as much on sea as on land and the football stadium of the University of Washington has docks for spectators who come by boat—and there was the threadlike grace of the Evergreen Floating Bridge. The air hostess, as usual, did not know its name, but kindly went to ask the pilot. We turned in over the famous Space Needle of last year's World's Fair—it almost put its orange head in at my starboard window—and there we were on the Boeing Air Field, where the enormous jets are made.

And of course it began to rain.

Our hotel, the Hilton Inn, is more than usually comfortable, which is saying a good deal.

I ought to make a photograph some time or other of the rows and rows of colored pennons which are a feature of U. S. gas stations. They look fine in a wind.

5 · 11 · 63

The rest of yesterday evening was a fine lazy time in the luxurious Hilton bedroom, watching hootnannies (sing-songs), etc., on the *TV*. I learned that the impetuous Mme. Nhu—her husband and brother-in-law assassinated—was holed up in the hotel where we had dinner with Julie. I also learned of *tab-opening cans*. You can now open a beer can, and, it is to be hoped, you will soon be able to open any other can, without a tin opener. Watching a Western movie, I reflected how important it was to know what sort of West? The West stretches from the snowy mountains where we are now to the Mojave desert where we were so recently, and no "cowboy" film can be authentic unless it is rigidly true to its own environment. I also pondered the following facts. 1) Nobody in a "Western" does any work. 2) The scenery is generally beautiful. 3) There seem to be lots of people about. (In real life, the bearded old characters slaved at their labor in frightful heat or cold, in desert landscapes which were practically unpopulated.) 4) Everybody is "on his honor"—in reality the law was the gun. 5) Everybody is rather well dressed with particularly well-tailored buttocks—in fact, most forty-niners must have been in tatters. 6) The well-fed blood horses of the movie world must really have been skin and bone.

Will anybody ever make a film about the real grandeur and toil and suffering and dauntless persistence of the pioneers who managed to survive?

This morning we went shopping at the Pike Street Market and at the Old Curiosity Shop, as it seemed to me that my kind Carol must be getting little fun out of a series of lectures and studies of geography. She bought, as usual, lots of presents for lots of friends and nothing for herself.

Then we took the ferry boat to Winslow, feeling that the proper feeling for Seattle must come from the sea. The weather forecast had been rain, so the sun came out for us.

The *surprise* of great mountains! I had been looking all about me for Mt. Rainier, the second highest peak in the U. S. (we have seen the highest, Mt. Whitney) when there it was, leaning over my shoulder. The reaction is, "Good God, it's a mountain!" (I.e., not a cumulus cloud which the eye had been skipping.) It is a wondrous ice-cream cone, once a volcano whose crater has collapsed inwards these billion years to make an internal lake of ice.

I had a good hot apple pie with cinnamon on the ferry. The apples of Washington are the best in the U. S.

At about 4:30, Professor Wendell Phillips and his wife came to pick us up. The first thing I discovered about this delightful Jew was that his name was Adrian, upon which I had to shake him warmly by the hand a second time—and then explain as best I could to him (a one-time rabbi) that Hadrian had not been such a monster as is believed by some Hebrews.

They took us to see some curiosa of Seattle in the gathering darkness—the Kent Puyallup Valley with its interesting garbage-disposal system, where employees of the Boeing Company (65,000 people said to earn $2,000,000 a day in wages) spend part of their time as moonlighters. They either grow rhubarb or daffodils or let the land lie fallow and appreciate in value. He told me that some Negro family got shot at lately hereabouts, without injury.

They took us to dine at their own shoreside wooden house, with a wonderful view up the sound over the shoulder of a big madrona tree at sea level. The waves lapped below us. Their dog was called Ack-Ack.

Professor Phillips advised me to read *Inside U.S.A.* by John Gunther and *The Immense Journey* by Norman Eisley.

The lady who introduced me at the lecture—which seemed to go down well—revealed a piece of news to me in her speech, that Wace (of the Arthurian myths) was born in Jersey!

6 · 11 · 63

We left Seattle at 8:45 A.M. in a Boeing 720 on our journey of 1,329 miles. For some reason the office had routed us through San Francisco (702 miles) toward which we sped over Salem at 600 m.p.h., eating our breakfast six miles up.

It was a cloudy day, with too few glimpses of the fascinating world below us. American nimbus clouds with the sun behind them seem to me to have an odd tinge of some special blue not seen in Europe. It may be cobalt with a touch of black in it, or French ultramarine with perhaps the smallest speck of rose madden.

There was a longish wait at San Francisco, of which I took advantage to hobble down and photograph Bufano's very interesting statue of the Madonna. It is in disgrace at present for looking, from behind, rather like a penis, but the mixture of mosaic, metal and enamel of its front, and the four-eyed Infant, with double-colored toes, are well worth consideration. The back is also reminiscent of the habit of a nun.

Our DC-8. left at 1 P.M. for Salt Lake City (627 miles) and the mysterious Mormons!

There were rectangular fertile fields after the coast range, snatches of their geometry through clouds. There were wrinkled fields like contour maps, which in fact their strata made them. High nimbus of a rainy day blotted most out. At 1:30 there was a lake and snow on a mountain. More alto stratus or cirrus. Desert mountains. A distant one to port with snow on it. Then 10/10ths cloud over the Great Salt Desert, much to my regret. Our shadow flew beside us *with its vapor trail,* a horizontal streak on the dim cloud.

As we descended through the thick stuff there was suddenly a sight or two of the putty-colored earth, then a strange infernal view of a serpentine desolate river (the Jordan); then, beneath wispy clouds, the great salty puddled plain with snowcapped mountains framing its terrible inhospitality. The flat skin of this version of the world is like a bather's on whose gray hide the salt has dried in rings. It must once have been the bottom of some great lake or sea, and it has the bones of dinosaurs in it.

We arrived tired at our splendid hotel, to find three odious letters waiting for us—one from the agent and two gleefully enclosed by him, from un-fans who considered the lectures too "popular." The complaint of one lady was that I had said there were 24 volumes in the Dictionary of National Biography when everybody knew there were only 12.

The exhaustion and sense of being stabbed in the back by people who had pretended to be friendly were not helped by the discovery—without the least warning from the agent—that I had to address an audience of *twelve thousand!*

7 · 11 · 63

Criticism is always worth attending to, even if you reject it after attention, or make some slight or great concession to it. After a certain amount of courtesy to those who met us, and two interviews with reporters, I tottered out last night to see what little I could of Salt Lake City. On my tired mind was the venom of the letters, and the Tabernacle which we tried to see was just shut. It was plain to a confused brain that the two complaints had come from eggheads, but that audiences of 12,000 were not composed of eggheads. I could only do the best I could for the average person. I stayed up late reading the *Book of Mormon* and all the literature I could find about Utah and wondering how on earth you spoke to 12,000 or established any intimacy with them. What can you tell 12,000 people? Can you tell them about yourself? Can you make risqué jokes about Richard Burton—particularly to Latter-day Saints who do not smoke or drink or take any stimulants or wear practically any color but black? (I had hastily changed into my black suit.) I did not show the letters to Carol, for fear of depressing her.

This morning Mr. Workman came to drive us to the huge University at Provo, an hour's drive toward the glorious mountain called Timpanogos under which the University nestles, and I went hangdog and exhausted to my doom.

The vast proceedings began with two hymns and ended with a blessing, delivered by a most beautiful girl with a lovely voice. It was partly a blessing on me, so simply and touchingly and affectionately delivered that I wanted to cry. The question period afterwards, in a smaller building, had people standing. The dean, who is lovingly known as the Old Dean of the Mountains, insisted on driving back to the hotel with us as a passenger. In between, so he kept telling us again and again, God bless him, it had been one of the best lectures they had ever had.

It seems that you treat 12,000 people as one.

I got Carol to do a broadcast with me in the afternoon, after which I have taken an hour's peace to write this, and the entries of the last two days. There is another lecture this evening at eight, within the Temple Square, to 2,000 only, and we were expected by our itinerary to leave for Chicago at breakfast time tomorrow. But we have so fallen in love with Salt Lake City that we have managed to alter the schedule and give ourselves another full day of Joseph Smith and Brigham Young. My pen is itching to begin on them, but they deserve a long, long entry to themselves, which must be left till tomorrow.

The dean had made me so happy that I showed the letters to Carol, who was furious. I said, Don't answer them. She said, Well, if he says anything to *me* about it I will, I can't help it.

Now a shower and a change of clothes and a different lecture, and tomorrow something of the stunning saga of this good, living, disciplined, industrious theocracy whose symbol is a beehive.

We have been showered with presents. The dean gave a bound history of the college with my name stamped on it. One of the lovely girls came up and gave me the *Book of Mormon,* also the *Doctrine and Covenants* and the *Pearl of Great Price.*

They are a proselytizing faith, as what living faith isn't?

I have tried to smoke as little as possible, and never on the streets or on a campus or of course in the grounds of the Temple.

8 · 11 · 63

For the last few journeys my mind has been boiling with the terrific epics of the conquest of the West—which ought to have their Prescott but have instead been murdered by Hollywood Westerns and Walt Disney fantasies.

But we were up at 8 A.M. and sightseeing till 7 P.M., so how can I summon the energy to start on it now, at 9:30?

I had better leave the story of the Mormons till I can

sort it out at leisure in Alderney, from books, and simply write down what we actually did today.

Dr. Bennion, a representative of one of the great original families which marched here with Brigham Young, took us with infinite patience and pride and information on the long all-day tour. We went first to the biggest copper mine in the world, then to the desert hills beyond Camp Floyd, then to the monument on the spot where the leader first looked down on the land which was to become Salt Lake City, and finally to the Beehive House (the leader's residence) and to the Tabernacle in Temple Square.

Here are some of the notes scribbled in my pocket book while Dr. Bennion talked to us:

His own grandfather, John Bennion, arrived in Utah on October the 5th, 1847. His grandmother used to help in herding the cattle. One day, when they were getting away from her, she set down her baby near a big sage bush to run after them. Having turned them, she realized she could not remember which of the myriad bushes it was. She, a short woman, was running about lamenting when a mounted man happened by. He galloped around looking for the baby from the height of horseback, found it for her, and scooped it up "in real cowboy fashion." This baby was Dr. Bennion's father. The adventure took place in Brigham Canyon. (We were driving through all this, the vast emptiness of almost waterless plain.)

The copper mine, in the mountain, an open pit of enormous size exactly like something out of Dante's *Inferno,* only yielded 3 percent of copper at the start, now only yields 75/100ths of 1 percent. Mormons *have always been willing to accept a subsistence level and to exploit it by industriousness.* Brigham Young himself accepted the desolate plain to establish his community *because nobody else would care to take it.* Then the industry and ingenuity of his people was set to work in every possible exploitation, from clay houses (adobe, here called 'dobie) to silkworms and anything else that could be tried. All the prophet asked his emissaries to find was three things: land, water and timber for fuel. All were distributed free, but rationed.

At first there was a little gold to be found—fortunately not much, or the Mormons might not have been let alone.

Dr. Bennion had himself been a cowhand before he took to education. He had had to herd his cattle 30 miles from Bennion Ranch to Camp Floyd without water in the summer drive, starting at 2 A.M. The cattle would smell water four miles off, at the end of the drive, and start to bellow and run. Cattle, he said, have different bellows which a cowboy can understand—a cattle language. When one of them died on the dreadful march they had a mourning cry for the dead one, like humans lamenting.

The Salt Lake corresponds to the Dead Sea in Palestine, Utah Lake to the Sea of Galilee, and between them in both cases runs the Jordan River. But as to running, the order is back to front, i.e. the Utah Jordan runs in the opposite direction to the Jewish one.

We traveled part of our journey along the old pony express road which had covered 1,800 miles (eventually run by Wells Fargo) from St. Joseph to Sacramento.

When Brigham Young outspanned at noon on July 24, 1847, they plowed the land, breaking the plows, and planted their stock of potatoes *before lunch.* The margin for getting a crop to feed on was as narrow as that. The (late) potatoes never did grow to a good size and for some time they fed themselves on the sego lily root, shown to them by an Indian chief called Washakie. This is the same as the camassia lily we heard about before. Its bulb is as big as a cherry, sweet, and has good protein value. By winter he had 3,000 people here, and 5,000 acres set with winter wheat. There *was* grass for the cattle. They nearly lost their crop to a plague of crickets, but sea gulls arrived from the Salt Lake and helped to check it. Ever since, the sea gull has been the sacred bird of the Mormons, as the beehive is their emblem and the lily their flower.

This bit of ecology is not romantic myth. Dr. Bennion had seen the same thing on his own father's ranch. When you make green a patch of the desert, the crickets do flock to it. The Bennion family had tried to combat them with fire, with banging cans, with trenches of water, with boards to strike them. (The dead were fed to the chickens.) Eventually, in Bennion's case also, the gulls had turned the scale.

The local Indians were branches of the Ute tribe—Gosiute, Paiute etc. They "don't do much of anything."

Early quarriers or masons cracked rock by boring holes, filling with water and waiting for it to freeze.

Out of 80,000 immigrants before the railway came in 1869, 6,000 were buried along the trail.

Mormons have always been liberal to other religions. Brigham Young himself gave the land for the Catholic Cathedral. There was once a rip-roaring mining camp of Catholics who heard they were going to be visited by their bishop but had no church and could not sing the mass. So their Mormon neighbors furnished their own tabernacle and the choir to sing it.

We heard the full story of the Mountain Meadow Massacre —a story of bad communications by horseback news. The overall situation was that the Mormons had been persecuted half across a continent, had begun to make good in this poverty-stricken refuge, but had merely been suspected of being in rebellion against the rest of America. President Buchanan had sent two armies against them. There was fear and misunderstanding on both sides when a wagon train passed on the way to California, having come from the very region where Joseph Smith had been shot. A fast pony message was sent to the prophet to seek instructions, but before the answer could arrive the local mob-situation had deteriorated. Mormons collaborated with Indians in a massacre of the wagon train—about 140 persons, all killed except 14 children. Then the answer arrived, a command to be peaceable. The Mormon leader sat down and wept. After some further maneuvers and scorched-earth policies against the invading armies, common sense prevailed with Buchanan's generals. (Not before the whole population of Salt Lake City had withdrawn to Provo, leaving their horses ready to be fired by themselves.) The blame for the massacre was fastened on a certain John D. Lee, who was executed at the place of the massacre as a scapegoat. The Mormons were said to have tricked the wagoners to lay down their arms, then attacked themselves, disguised as Indians. I must read a book about this called *John D. Lee* by Juanita Brooks, a sequel to her *Mountain Meadows Massacre.*

The Beehive House is a magnificent piece of Victoriana. The Long Hall would send John Betjeman frantic with delight. Its furniture, Franklin stoves, etc., are authentic. At the end of our tour we were given candies of horehound and peppermint from the storeroom whence the prophet supplied his families.

From this storeroom there developed the idea of the first department store in the U. S. (Zion's Cooperative Mercantile Institution) which I photographed. It and our (Idaho) hotel behind it make a wonderful group of early twentieth-century architecture.

We went over the Tabernacle, next to the building where I lectured last night, and heard its organ and acoustics. Its beams are pegged with wood or secured with thongs.

The stone for the Temple was dragged 20 miles by oxen because only stone was good enough for their angel, Moroni.

Marriage among Mormons is for eternity—not "till death do us part"—but divorce is possible, though difficult.

I am really too exhausted to write more, and have to fly to Chicago tomorrow, rising at 5:45.

The Mormon adieu is "You Bet!" It used to be "You betcha life!" It sounds like, "Yew baiet."

9 • 11 • 63

So we were off again for the same sort of distance as the Pony Trail of the forty-niners from St. Joseph to Sacramento—the same sort of route that the Mormons took in their hated-by-others trek from Illinois. It was Illinois we were going to. In a couple of hours we were to cover the calvary which took them three months or six. Many of them did it with *handcarts* only—no wagons at all.

In the dawn, in the bowl of grim snowy mountains round the salty plain, I could not help thinking of Brigham Young's arrival there and of Browning's Childe Roland.

> I saw them and I knew them all and yet
> Dauntless the slug horn to my lips I set
> And blew, Childe Roland to the Dark Tower came!

We had a 720 jet which did the 1,290 miles between 7:30 and 10:10—which the Time Line converted to 11:10. It was cloudy.

At 8:20 some vast baked mud puddle showed through the cirrus. Later came a lunar landscape, not one human habitation from horizon to horizon and just one thread of road. Later still there were corduroy fields in a terracelike pattern, long narrow strips. These multiplied till we had a patchwork quilt of striped linens. I have not seen these bar-of-chocolate fields elsewhere. Then there were small frozen or ice-rimmed lakes like a white pox. Cloud again. (In their fearful journey westward the Saints had their own poor brass band! It earned a little money along the way. They sang their own hymn, "All is well, all is well!") Next came the endless central chessboard of patchwork of agriculture, with its straight-ruled roads. Most U. S. fields are inclined to be more long than wide. It must have something to do with turning the tractor plow.

It fills me with despair that I have not done justice to the Saints. In fact, none of this journal does justice to anybody or anywhere. We skim along, six miles up, often very tired, and are gone before we have really made contact. (But how can you talk of being tired compared with those handcart men?)

A book like this can only be superficial. The alternative is to write 15 volumes on each subject and spend a lifetime on it. (Memo: get the 15 volumes of *Far West and the Rockies,* by Dr. and Mrs. LeRoy R. Hafen, historians whom I met yesterday.) The most impressive sight in Salt Lake City was the worn clumsy wooden roadmeter whose geared wheels measured their splendid journey.

Although we are now in Chicago, the second largest city in America, with a population 50 percent colored, I can't help going on thinking about the Mormons. For a few hours we have been living in a stern and contented and self-denying theocracy *which works,* whose members aid one another on principle. Whatever you may feel about the Angel Moroni and his golden book (which was returned to him), whatever you may feel about the Victorian furniture of Brigham Young's house (which, incidentally, was humped across a continent and the house built in a year—out of nothing), whatever sort of religion you may have yourself, you can't get away from the humble pride and courage and grandeur of this achievement. I said that Disneyland came out of the brain of one man. What a mouse's fart it seems beside the whole of Utah, which came out of the brain of Brigham Young.

The skyscrapers of Chicago are spiry—a spiry metropolis, but not branchy between spires. There are two nice round skyscrapers, a better idea than matchbox ones. The city has a lot of splendid American-Victorian domestic architecture. It offers a variant hitherto unknown to me, *Rusticated* Gothic.

10 · 11 · 63

To my mind the greatest wonders we have seen in Chicago are the Thorne Rooms at the Art Institute. These miniature rooms, of which there are about fifty done to the scale of one inch to the foot, are the lifework of a rich lady called Mrs. James Ward Thorne, who is still living. Instead of collecting dollhouse furniture she employed "a corps of expert craftsmen who developed their unique abilities under Mrs. Thorne's direction over a period of more than a decade." They are infinitely superior to the famous Queen's Doll's House in England, their period exactitude is faultless to the scholar of furniture, and, to the author of *Mistress Masham's Repose*, they were an enchantment. It seems a little whimsical to mention the following facts against their background of *scholarship*, but the knitting cast down on a table by some housewife disturbed at our intrusion is actual knitting done on pin-sized knitting needles—the clocks wind—the tiny chessmen can be moved—there are needlepoint Oriental rugs—some inhabitants have left their spectacles or a copy of a newspaper on the sofa (in one English case, *Country Life*)—and, in a seafaring interior from Cape Cod, there is a miniature ship in a miniature bottle, the whole perhaps less than half an inch long. Miniature dollhouses generally have an air of slight clumsiness by which they can be detected at once. The rugs are just that fraction too thick or the legs of the chairs seem too massive. If these rooms were magnified twelve times, they would be indistinguishable from real rooms. On top of that, they are utterly correct to their own period. (It seems madly ungrateful to point out the smallest defect, but there is one small one. The sun lights most of the windows from both sides of the room. No doubt this was done to give a full light to the furniture, but it disturbs an artist's eye.) In one of the cabinets, a secretary, even the secret drawers can be opened!

In one of the English interiors, just to emphasize the eerie luck which follows me, Carol spotted a bust of Antinoüs in the hallway outside.

American interiors have always depended on a greater use of wood than is common in England. I mean unvarnished and unpainted wood with less upholstery, less ornament and perhaps less comfort. At least Carol says it looks less comfortable.

Surely, at night, when the public is excluded—*pace* the whims of Walt Disney—there *must* be a society of international Lilliputians, including American ones (and Lilliput originally existed off the northwest coast of America) to take advantage of these superb homes.

We drove around Chicago in a cab to get such photographs as we might. The driver told us that the Windy City is so windy that in winter gales they have to fit ropes along the lake front for the wayfarers to steady themselves on.

The skyscrapers all seem to have put more effort into adorning their tops than the New York ones have. The Tribune Tower is a little like our favorite General Electric in New York, though much more massive. The circular motels are excellent. The American Victorian domestic architecture is perhaps more individual than in any other place we have visited, more rampageous, and the famous Water Tower—

one of the few survivors of the great fire—is in a fine variant of Rusticated Gothic Fort.

In the afternoon we felt it our duty to go to see *How the West Was Won* on Cinerama, we having just returned from those parts and full of their epic interest.

There is something wrong with this film which we can't quite define. It is as if it had been written and directed by several people. One of its authors has made a sincere effort not to be sentimental, not to be unfair to the Indians, and not to be too scenic. (The deserts we have viewed were not "scenery." Another has insisted on at least two love interests. Another has chosen shots beautifully framed by trees. Another has introduced the usual battle scenes which bear no relation to the Civil War and the usual fight on a runaway train. Another, evidently an existentialist, has made it clear that Natural Selection made it inevitable for the railway to oust the Indian and the buffalo. There is no central unity. It is not *half* as bad as it might have been from Metro-Goldwyn-Mayer, but somehow it is a forgettable movie.

It is too scenic, too patriotic, too boy-meets-girl.

Yet, if Americans are sentimental, which, bless them, they are, perhaps it is true in its own way. It certainly moved my own simpler sentiments, but then I am half an American already.

One point it did bring home to me.

I have been partly overestimating the grandeur of the wagon trains. If you have a thoroughly organized train, with water carried, stops properly arranged, beef on the hoof, access to buffalo and expert planning, then it must be possible to cross even the Mojave desert with little more than tedium and endless labor. But who crossed it first? It is the Mountain Men, the trappers, the explorers, the Indians themselves, that I have been forgetting.

Ultimately *who,* what single human soul alone, can possibly have traversed the *months* of Rockies, the *ages* of forest, the *aeons* of desert which can be practically pure cement?

How the West Was Won really ought to have been about humanity, about the anthropoid, about the astonishing spirit of surmounting Man. Personally I think that men are a hateful species of animal, but you do have to hand it to their indomitable endurance.

11 · 11 · 63

A sunny, wintry Veterans Day.

We left the somehow Teutonic rustications of Chicago by train for a change, departing from a titanic railway station like the Baths of Caracalla in Rome. American termini, I mean the actual platforms at which the trains end their journeys, seem to be all grimy darkness under shafts of light. We had about 230 miles to cover, via Springfield to Jacksonville.

There were miles and miles of industrial plants painted silver in complex shapes of science fiction, and here and there the pink granite or rough-hewn churches which will one day be as acceptable as the colonial spires of Massachusetts. The trees around Chicago were now sure that winter had come.

After an hour or so we were among the vast fields of sweet corn, stubble, winter wheat and soya bean which form the flat Middle West. The Goddess of Chicago is Ceres, our cabdriver had informed us, pointing to her statue on the Chamber of Commerce. As usual, nobody was in the fields.

We noticed from the train window, not for the first time, that Americans have a yen for using painted carriage wheels as decoration; also, that no American railway station ever seems to have a visible name on it. The signposting on roads is also inferior to the signposting in Britain.

The trees had decided that it was still the fall in Springfield.

Dr. Blair, the dean of MacMurray College, met us at the station and kindly drove us round the town to see and photograph the house which President Lincoln had lived in. Our schedule is too tight to allow us to visit New Salem, where the log houses and their furniture have been restored to the condition they were in at the time of Lincoln.

The dean, a Methodist, told us of a Methodist bishop in Chicago who had been asked to go to Birmingham (Alabama) to join in a protest against the exclusion of Negroes from white churches. The bishop, born in the South, had replied, "I may go to Hell, but I won't go to Birmingham." So a Catholic monsignor went instead. What complicates the story is that the monsignor had not been born in the South.

Jacksonville has a typical Midwestern town square, with a statue in the middle, and was once a station on the underground escape route for slaves. The brother of Harriet Beecher Stowe (*Uncle Tom's Cabin*) was president of a college here.

Methodist ministers are going to Birmingham on a weekly rota, to get arrested for trying to take colored people to church with them. Hence the Bishop Who Wouldn't.

Lincoln, who was born and educated in great poverty hereabouts, had a kind, ugly face, and it was due to his honest and painful persistence that the United States are United still. His honesty was such that when he had overcharged some woman a few cents, while working in a store, he walked many miles through wild country to pay her back. I forget how many.

That's the trouble about this journal, nothing gets verified before you are off elsewhere.

The lecture, to a sparse audience because the advertising had mentioned the wrong day, was a modest success. About twenty boys and girls kept me talking till 10:30, two hours after it had finished. The college is another of these examples of the American Renaissance, whose numbers have doubled since 1955. Its benefactor or local Grand Duke was a president of the Acme Steel Corporation called Senator MacMurray. We dined with Mrs. Michalson, the president's wife, and some of the faculty, including the charming Dr. Rose who introduced the lecture. As usual everybody was more than kind.

I must find out more about Lincoln, who seems to have got rather a dirty deal out of life, as most good men do.

12 · 11 · 63

Lincoln said: "May our children and our children's children to a thousand generations continue to enjoy the benefits conferred upon us by a united country." A thousand generations would be about 25,000 years, considerably longer than all the dynasties of Egypt, so I doubt if this wish will be fulfilled.

It has been a tiring day with little to show for it.

We left by bus at 9:30, caught the Abraham Lincoln train for Chicago at 10:45, found that our 720 jet from Chicago to Pittsburgh had been delayed by bad weather on the West Coast, and finally got to our hotel in Pittsburgh by the delayed jet at about 8:30. So, in eleven hours of travel and waiting, by bus, train and aircraft, we have only covered about 651 miles.

We arrived in the dark. All I know of Pittsburgh is that it is the center of the steel industry, that it was named after Pitt (but whether the Elder or the Younger, I don't know), and that the view of its lighted jewel box by night as you drop down into its river valley and cross the bridge is of absolutely breathtaking magnificence.

Our train to Chicago, as yesterday, was of the Gulf, Mobile and Ohio R.R. (I really must find out about the railway sagas.) We noticed again as we traversed the infinite plain of agriculture how *clean* American farms are compared with British ones—their homesteads, silos, rails, ornamental carriage wheels, all freshly whitewashed. In 421 miles we actually saw three humans working tractors in the fields.

At Joliet, nearing Chicago, there seemed to be some sort of factory done up rather engagingly as Hampton Court, in yellow stone. Why not? I find it difficult to convince Americans that I am not teasing them when I admire their architectural adventures. I like their Gothic as much as I like Horace Walpole's, and that is very much indeed. We got a splendidly mad photograph of a church in Springfield which had suddenly taken it into its head to be a fort for toy Bavarian soldiers.

The reason for the illegibility of American road signs, and also names of stations, must be that the prevalence of other advertisements overpowers and upstages them.

A typical American gesture of cabdrivers, never seen in Britain, is the glance over the shoulder (not in the driving mirror) to make sure on freeways what sort of traffic is behind or overtaking or merging.

Tomorrow I have to lecture, morning and afternoon, to the University of Pittsburgh, which styles itself "the Cathedral of Learning" and whose benefactor was apparently Carnegie. All this I must investigate before the lectures.

In the evening we have a great treat.

13 · 11 · 63

If Beckford's romantic dream of Fonthill was worth erecting, which it certainly was, then Pittsburgh's Cathedral of Learning, which has the same feeling, was worth erecting too. I thought, before they took me over it, that it was merely an American Gothic cathedral, i.e. for church services. But oh, no, you can trust my adored Americans to be sentimental as all hell, with a simplicity and innocence and romanticism that you can't help loving and praising and wanting to protect. In short, the University of Pittsburgh came to the conclusion that Learning was a holy thing which deserved to be worshiped nondenominationally for its own sake and built this skyscraper of a cathedral not to God but to Knowledge. It has no altars. It wastes space with a magnificent prodigality—not wastes it, but dedicates it to culture or art or knowledge or beauty or whatever you like to call it. The impression it gives is strangely like the impression which must actually have been given by cathedrals in the Middle Ages, when they were *used* by people. There is a monkish coming and going.

The "cathedral" itself is at this moment valued for insurance purposes at $30,000,000. Its idea was conceived in the 1920's, somewhere around 1925, by the then chancellor Dr. J. G. Beauman and a Mrs. Ruth Crawford Mitchell, and it was gradually put up during the Depression and dedicated in 1937.

Around the central hall there are nineteen lecture rooms, each one ornamented and furnished in the style of a different country—Chinese, French, Yugoslav, etc.

The benefactors or Medicean Grand Dukes connected with the enterprise were diverse. Sometimes a lecture room was given by the government concerned. Some of the money came from people like Mellon or Carnegie. Some came from the students themselves. The furniture and detail is sumptuous for a classroom which is actually in use—we could not visit several of them for that reason—and there is no vandalism. The students are proud of their International Rooms, as they call them, and have treated them with respect. I am certain that elegance helps learning and that you learn better French, and are indeed a better person, if you learn it in a room with a Gobelin tapestry.

The English International Room contained features salvaged from the House of Commons after the Germans had bombed it, and the Union Jack hangs there, to my great pleasure, beside the Stars and Bars.

In the Irish Room there was a copy of the *Book of Kells* and an easy Gaelic inscription which anybody could put into English: do ċum zlóire dé azus onóra na L-Éireann.

Now it is easy to make a cheap, eggheaded sneer about the romanticism of this concept—you have only to use the word *whimsy*—and no doubt everybody did sneer at Beckford's Fonthill. Some of the detail may be idealized, unlike Mrs. Thorne's detail but like a boy's dream of the Hunchback of Notre Dame or the Three Musketeers or Ivanhoe. I like boys, I like all young people, and I am a romantic. The children who are acquiring merit here are acquiring idealism too, which is not a bad thing to acquire whatever its weaknesses, and I cannot write too often that it is a good thing that millionaires should expend their ill-gotten gains on culture. The Cathedral of Knowledge has some of the grandiose inutility of the Washington Monument, which is 90,000 tons of stone dedicated to nothing but ornament, but this is a noble dedication, not a silly one. We have had quite enough functionalism and utility and existentialism in my lifetime, quite enough gabble about the beauty of quadrilateral skyscrapers like matchboxes stood on end. The boys who have studied at Pittsburgh will leave the place as sentimentalists and dreamers and do-gooders. Well, I had rather have them than Machiavellians and costing clerks and do-badders. The human race is quite foul enough, as Graham Greene ought to know, without insisting that it should pursue its foulness with even greater sincerity. Cathedrals of Learning are more viable socially than Stock Exchanges.

In the evening we went to see one of the touring companies of *Camelot* at the Nixon Theatre. We have been whizzing round the U. S. at 600 m.p.h., while two touring companies of my beloved musical have been plodding round beneath us, with seven freight cars of scenery and dresses. This is the first time we have both played in the same town and been free to visit each other.

It was the company which had Louis Hayward, Jan Moody and Arthur Treacher for its stars, also an excellent youth called Robert Peterson as Lancelot.

I saw *Camelot* about seventy times three years ago, from various parts of the house and wings and dressing rooms, and it was eerie to see it again, now polished like a stone which has been three years under the waterfall, and to find that the whole lovable cast was still worrying about the very same problems that the original cast of Richard Burton, Julie Andrews and Robert Goulet used to worry about. The cast has always loved and worried about the play as if it were a child of its own. The central problem remains the same as it always was. *Camelot* is not a musical comedy like *My Fair Lady*, it is a musical tragedy. The audience, though it does laugh a good deal, goes away in tears. I personally wept four times, with the regularity of an alarm clock. This baffles the audience, the critics and the actors. Why are we not laughing as at *My Fair Lady*? Well, the answer is that it ought not to be judged by its laughs, but by its silences and tears. The music is thirty times better than *My Fair Lady's* (not so catchy) and the actors, although they did have to follow the genius of Richard and Julie, were thoroughly adequate. I cried in the same places.

After the performance I was asked backstage to meet the assembled cast, and showed them my tears, and told them how polished they were, and I hope I gave them a little encouragement in the slightly bad patch they had struck at Pittsburgh, through being there a week too long. (Numerical source of audience overestimated.) There were only two members of the original cast that I could recognize, plus the amiable stage manager, Ed Preston.

14 · 11 · 63

The usual trek from Pittsburgh to Columbus, Ohio, in a Constellation at 8,000 ft. It took us about 45 minutes and must have been approximately 150 miles. We were over cloud most of the time and a warning to pilots was out, about not running into migrating swans whose peak of migration will be reached on Friday.

Columbus is memorable for two rivers with fine Indian names (Olentangy and Scioto) and for being the hometown of James Thurber (whose "Day the Dam Broke" is an actual piece of Columbus history) and for having had among its benefacting Grand Dukes a gentleman called Schumacher, who made the memorable discovery that if you put alcohol in your medicines during a time of prohibition you made your fortune. The Gallery of Fine Arts in which I spoke was largely due to him.

The Crichton Club to which I spoke and with which we banqueted and held a reception was founded in 1919 and has grown to be an expensive, upper-class, much-sought-after institution which has three guest speakers a year. I noticed Aldous Huxley and Sir John Gielgud among the many distinguished visitors who had signed the book. We dressed for dinner, I am glad to say, and everything was civilized and pleasant and as warmhearted as ever.

The last two lectures have been successful. This was a difficult one to succeed in, as it was to adults. I can generally charm the young, but grown-ups are less easy to deceive! They claimed, however, that I had deceived them to their satisfaction, and the reception line afterwards kept me standing on the leg which couldn't be insured against loss of employment until 11:30. The critical standard of the club was higher than what I usually have to face. After all, where Louis Hayward was having to follow Richard Burton, I was having to follow Aldous Huxley.

This is an inadequate entry about Columbus, but it is hard work keeping the journal up-to-date. I am taking in or giving out so much, so hard, so long. Our benefactors here were Mr. and Mrs. Matthews.

15 · 11 · 63

This was one of our terrific days, but it is getting on for midnight and we must be off to New Orleans at 7 A.M. tomorrow, i.e. get up then. Anyway, it may be better to recollect it in tranquility.

16 · 11 · 63

We flew to Cincinnati, say 100 miles at 8,000 ft. over cloud, in a seventeen-year-old Convair 240, whose stewardess told me about their catering arrangements, etc. I asked why I was not allowed to smoke while their ovens had the electricity on. She said the ovens are switched off during takeoff and landing. She also said that the pilots and copilots were not allowed to eat the same meals. This was due to the fact that some time ago there was a case of food poisoning in the cockpit and the aircraft was barely able to make a forced landing before both pilots passed out.

Well, our very happy day in Delaware yesterday was due to the thoughtfulness of Dr. and Mrs. Marshall of the Wesleyan (Ohio) University. He came to collect us at noon, drove us by non-freeway roads to Delaware, stopped for us to photograph hex signs on Mennonite barns in Stratford, showed us the rather English countryside of this region where the wealth is more evenly distributed than anywhere else in the States, and entertained us to a delicious meal in his museum of a house. It was a rather Charles Addams structure, with cast-iron ornamental tracery on its porch, and furnished with just the sort of Victorian lavishness which appeals to me. After luncheon his colored maid, Mrs. Elvira Beasley, sang two spirituals in the genuine, extemporary Negro mode, not the popular Paul Robeson stuff. But the great interests he had provided were for the afternoon and evening.

He took us to three fraternity houses and one sorority.

The young men and women were delighted to welcome us and show us over.

It seems that a fraternity house, which is distinguished by various Greek letters from the other fraternities, has about 45 denizens who are composed of seniors, juniors and sophomores. These are served by about 16 freshmen, who wear red caps and whose duty it is to clean the living rooms, wait on table and call their masters in the morning. The freshman, who has a special master, lives in a dormitory elsewhere and may have to get up and come over to the fraternity house as early as 5 A.M. to call his owner. He presents him with an engraved paddle, which has both their names on it, much more formidable than the joke one we bought in Spokane, and these are hung in a row on the walls of the dining room. Presumably they may be used in some form of initiation ceremony about which it seemed politer not to inquire.

The seniors, juniors and sophomores share rooms upstairs in the fraternity house, two or three to a room, and also sleep in dormitories upstairs, about seven to a dormitory. Their rooms are individual, untidy like the rooms of all adolescents, and ornamented with all kinds of private oddities. One had a tank of tropical fish in it, with a pinup girl in the nude behind its back wall, to cheer up the fish.

Each fraternity has a tie-pin with the mystic greek letters on it. When a member falls in love with a girl in a sorority, he presents her with his pin, a minor equivalent of the engagement ring. At a certain time, I think in the spring of the year, the whole fraternity dons formal dress with black ties and goes over at night to serenade the lucky lady. It is her duty to stand on the balcony of her sorority house, holding a candle during the serenade.

The sorority house we visited was organized in much the same way as the fraternity ones had been, but it was a purely social center and the pretty girls did not sleep in it.

The reason why the freshman has to come over to call his senior in the mornings is that if you have seven seniors sleeping in the same room you can't have seven alarm clocks without chaos.

Some houses are better cleaned than others and some have won more cups than others, of which they are proud, and each has a recognized character of its own—athletic, social, scholarly, etc.

There is one House brother to each fraternity. This has been found to work better than having a married couple. The boys suit the catering to their purses and there are two professional cooks.

We signed the visitors' book in each House.

The treat arranged for Carol in the evening was to dine alone with an entire fraternity in its House, chaperoned by Mrs. Marshall, while I ate elsewhere with faculty members. She says that the food was good, her hosts attentive, and that after dinner they all sang fraternity songs—ballads, as it were, celebrating the feasts and idiosyncrasies and adventures of their members. Each House has a large scrapbook also, which illustrates the history of the group with photographs.

The lecture in the evening was a full house of about 1,400 who gave us an ovation at the end. We adjourned to another building for questions, followed by practically the entire audience, as if I had been the Pied Piper. Dr. Ferguson told them so, pointing out that they were not however rats, and we actually disorganized a dance there—the first time, he said, that a lecturer had ever put to flight a jazz band. There were so many that eventually I had to shout my answers from halfway up a staircase, feeling as embarrassed as our Saviour must have done when they used to let down clients through the roof. Needless to say, I was thrilled by the youth, intelligence, generosity and enthusiasm—you could almost say affection—of this happy and excited throng. I signed books and bits of paper till the sponsors forced us to go away, leaving many unsatisfied, saying that it was unfair to keep us up longer when we had today's long journey to New Orleans in front of us.

I shall always remember the Wesleyans of Delaware with devotion, and try hard to go back there.

I write up this wonderful exchange of hearts and knowledge, quite inadequately, during the long wait at Cincinnati, about which I shall never know anything. But I will have left a great slice of my love in Ohio Wesleyan, and I have a buckeye chestnut in my pocket, to plant in Alderney.

17 · 11 · 63

First I must bring yesterday up-to-date.

There was some mechanical trouble afflicting Delta Airlines, at whose hands we flew about 100 miles from Columbus to Cincinnati in an ancient Convair, about 400 miles in another one from Cincinnati to Atlanta (with stops at Lexington and Chattanooga) and finally, in a DC-8 from Atlanta to New Orleans, about 400 miles more. What with delays at one stop followed by extreme haste at another, we did not reach New Orleans till 6:40 in the evening (5:40 by their time, as we had crossed another boundary of time) and, at that, the airline had lost our baggage for us.

Cincinnati to Lexington was rolling and ridgy, almost like very blistered paint or quilted upholstery or the marks round the edge of a piecrust. There were then the bigger, bluegrass fields of America's horse-breeding area, and it looked like what an Englishman would think to be fine fox-hunting country, say the vale of Aylesbury or even Leicestershire. There were low neat white walls around the water holes, to prevent the stock from puddling them up into mud.

Lexington to Chattanooga showed us that the trees were still considering it to be the fall, not winter yet. Here, all over the landscape—wait a bit, you can say "landscape" and "seascape"; there ought to be a word to describe the almost horizonless panorama from an aircraft—here, all over the earthscape, were the numerous mirrors of dew ponds. They made a texture almost like the Indian textiles of my babyhood, when small round mirrors were sewn into the material. Some large serpentine river (our maps are as usual inadequate airline folders) met us forty minutes from Chattanooga. At 4 P.M. there were wooded hills or mountains, I suppose the Smoky Mountains?

Chattanooga to Atlanta was an earthscape of low, wooded, rolling hills a bit like the lowlands of Scotland or Wales, part woodland, part agriculture. Somebody (in the North) told me that the South has exhausted its soil by planting too much tobacco and cotton without rotating the crops enough. Later it became more tree-filled and swampy, with lakes somehow spongy in outline, or like a vast river in currentless woody puddles.

From *Atlanta to New Orleans* (at 27,000 ft. in a jet at last) there was the orange spectrum of a medal-ribbon sunset over swampy lakes fretted like Chinese dragons, or like what I imagine the Everglades to be, and in these I suppose there were alligators and water moccasins. The resources, I was told by two Texans, were oil and fishing (shrimps). There was much zigzag water and what I took to be bayous.

We were met at New Orleans by Carol's godfather, Dr. Byron Unkauf, who has invited us to stay at his home. This is our first real visit with an American family, with Mrs. Unkauf and two boys at undergraduate age and a charming daughter of thirteen.

The children instantly adopted Carol and whisked her off to a fraternity dance, while Byron and Meryl Unkauf took me to dinner at the Commander's Palace, one of the best and most typical restaurants in New Orleans. The building dates from 1880, but had been burned down, except for the bar, in 1947. It has been restored to its former splendor, which includes a magnificent Victorian gas chandelier now adapted to electricity.

Our menu was hot garlic bread, shrimp rémoulade (the sauce made with tabasco), turtle soup (snappers?) and trout amandine with soufflé potatoes. I ate these because they were ordered for me, but have stuck to my vegetarianism when I order for myself.

After dinner we walked in the patio, where I saw for the

first time in real life the Spanish moss which grows on trees in romantic Southern movies. I was told that it is not parasitic to the tree (it draws its sustenance from the surrounding air) and that it only grows on "live oaks," i.e. the local evergreen oak. It is beautiful when lit from below, as it was in the patio. It was under the funereal moss of these live oaks in the City Park that the countless duels of old New Orleans used to be fought out.

Then they took me on a night tour of the garden district, showing me the wonderful and indigenous architecture of the South—a matter of cast-iron frills like lacework which rises to its greatest individuality in a few now rare cast-iron fences modeled on corn cobs. It is very beautiful.

At ten past twelve I tumbled into bed—no luggage—and was asleep when my head touched the pillow. We had touched Ohio, Kentucky, Tennessee, Georgia, Alabama, Mississippi and Louisiana.

I got up at 8 A.M. to write this and at 11 o'clock fulfilled one of my ambitions, to go to church with an American family. Carol and the other children stayed in bed to sleep off their night's revels while Meryl, Byron and I went to their Episcopalian service—identical with what the English call "C of E" except that the psalm was read instead of sung. Byron says that the U. S. Episcopalians have bishops but no archbishops and do acknowledge some sort of link with the Archbishop of Canterbury. The congregation was about 300.

We went on from church to "breakfast at Brennans," a habit in New Orleans. Our host was Mrs. Crager of the Lyceum which I am to address tomorrow and the meal extended from about 12:30 to 3:20. The menu, excellently cooked, began for one of the guests with "absinthe frappé" and went on through Eggs Nouvelle Orleans (poached eggs on blue crabs) to crêpes Suzette with chocolate sauce, bits of lemon rind and a white cream containing Grand Marnier. Evidently two of the products of the Deep South are cookery and leisure. Some people add drink and lovemaking. We bought one of the local pralines each in a shop afterwards. They are a sort of fudge poured over pecan nuts.

The shops, except the big stores,were open although it was Sunday. There were cabs and fringed surreys in the streets of the French Quarter, driven by Negroes in top hats. There were trams. There was a Rain Tree. Everywhere there was the graceful cast iron and wrought iron which makes New Orleans into a filigree city and branchy between metal bowers.

We went for a drive in the afternoon, to see the Mississippi and the lake on the opposite side of town with their levees—which are banks of faced soil to defend the lowland against flooding—and their bayous, which are acres of the lake or sea. We visited a cemetery to take photographs of the raised tombs. In this low-lying delta which may be seven feet below sea level, people have to be buried aboveground in their family mausoleums. Once in, they have to be left for a year and a day before the door can be opened again. If another member of the family dies before the required time, he has to serve his 366 days elsewhere, perhaps in somebody else's mausoleum.

The Unkaufs gave me their views on segregation as we drove. Byron says that time will *not* produce integration, that the races are dissimilar, that intermarriage is actually illegal in Louisiana, Mississippi, and Alabama, that there is more crime among colored people, and that he does not allow his wife or children out at night without an escort. He agrees that the Civil War is unforgotten and that the more the North presses for integration the more the South will resist it. He says that 40 percent of New Orleans is colored. He says there is a prevalence of juvenile delinquency and that Negroes will not attend their own schools. He says colored people are too "uninhibited." The public swimming pools have been closed here, rather than allow integration of them, and so they remain empty altogether.

Kennedy is disliked by the Unkaufs. The President's two problems here are integration and the discovery of some solution to the oil problem. This one is about territorial waters for oil drilling in the Gulf of Mexico.

Adults go to Sunday school.

From six till about ten past midnight there was a reception at the Unkauf's and perhaps the most interesting person I met was Paul McIlherry, the amusing owner of the estate where tabasco is manufactured (he is the sole proprietor of its secret) and which is a famous sanctuary for the snowy egret. He and Mrs. McIlherry and Laurraine Gorean, the columnist, and others, helped me to make a mournful list of some of the famous regional drinks which I might have sampled—Sazerac (a speciality of New Orleans, where, incidentally, the Cocktail was invented), tequila made from cactus, Boston Club Punch, corn whisky, mint julep, buttered rum (New England), rum Ramsay, and a Hurricane, which comes in a special glass like a hurricane lamp. You may keep the glass, or return it for a dollar. I think I will have to sample all of them simultaneously, the day after my last lecture.

We had a lot of interesting conversation and I learned a good deal, including the fact that the state laws of Louisiana are founded on the Napoleonic code. (By the way, apropos of conversation I see by the notebook that Dr. Marchall of Delaware suggested that Keats ought to be read in a cockney accent.)

The younger guests, Carol's friends, made me go and talk to them for half the time in a different room of this big house. We were fed on turkey and ham and local crayfish which finally proved it to the hilt, that New Orleans is the greatest town in America for the gourmet. (Brennan, the proprietor of the restaurant where we breakfasted yesterday, dropped dead at a Tostevin dinner.)

18 · 11 · 63

My mind is a perfect and absolute blank.

I remember I had a night's sleep and was not awakened till 9:30. I remember we went to the University at 11:30 to have lunch with the professors. I remember we recorded a TV appearance and a radio one (Carol was in the first of these). I remember we went looking for a walking stick in the curiosity shops with Willie B. Wisdom, having lost my dear old Dublin shillelagh yesterday. I remember we made a fairly sucessful lecture to a thin house in a big auditorium —it is difficult when an audience is spread out to move them as a unit. I remember the students kept me answering questions till about 11 P.M.

But the important thing is New Orleans. Its jazz, of which it is more or less the original home, in Preservation Hall at 726 St. Peter Street. Its Mardi Gras balls with the masked swains calling out their favored ladies to dance and awarding a favor to the first five. They carry these "crew favors" in a possibly velvet bag over the arm. Each ball is given by a "crew." (Last year Meryl got four silver spoons from a crew called the Caliphs of Cairo. Byron belongs to one called Osiris, as well as to the Caliphs. The oldest one, Comus, is over 100 years old. Nobody ever knows who the King of Comus is.) A good deal of drama can be attached to these gifts. Meryl told me that in the old days this was the way you paid your mistress—giving something of real value, perhaps title deeds or jewelry. . . .

22 · 11 · 63

I first heard of President Kennedy's assassination as I lay in hospital, with glucose and vitamins dripping into the veins of my left arm out of a yellow bottle and with a good many holes in my hide from hypodermics of morphia and antibiotics.

What an astonishing destiny for a simple human being! Was it a fortunate one? Was he one of "fortune's darlings"? What did he think of it in his private hours, if he thought at all or had any?

Born to enormous riches, educated at Harvard (where he was a pretty good swimmer), allowed as a Harvard junior to come down here to New Orleans for the thrill of Mardi Gras, amorous, lucky and courageous in war, either dedicated by his unpopular father to public life because an elder brother was dead or else bitten by the bug of public speaking as I have tardily been, astonishingly selected to perhaps the most powerful public office in the world, faced by fearsome decisions involving atomic war, hated by the Deep South, educated as a statesman while he went along (the youngest U. S. President), physically handicapped by spinal injury, rumored to be prepotent, spotlighted by day and night, a guard on his lips where none could really guard his life, never not the jeune premier, one of the three most important people in the world, and now murdered eleven years younger than I am—his birthday was the same day as mine—did he think he was making History or being made by it? What would his answer have been to Tolstoy, who thought that Napoleon was the slave of France and not her master? Did he think it had been worth it? Was he happy? How would he have gotten on with my emperor Hadrian?

I wonder what Madame Nhu is thinking about? What do great people think about? What does God think about?

26 · 11 · 63

It was interesting to lie in half a coma watching America adjust itself to the assassination. The first reaction was blank, like a jigsaw puzzler who holds a piece which won't fit in anywhere. Presidents had been assassinated, they knew, but that was history and somehow not here and now. It was Lady Macbeth's reaction. "What, in *our* house?" The second was the random suspicions and rumors. Everybody in the South said that the President had been warned repeatedly not to go to Texas, to wear a bulletproof vest, etc. There was a strong faction who thought his assassin (Oswald) had had to be silenced by the second man (Ruby) because it was a "gangland" murder, or a political one (Communist, Cuban?). There was even a prevalent rumor that Ruby had hanged himself in his cell. (It gradually became plain to my own mind that Oswald had been a crazy megalomaniac with persecution mania, operating on his own, and Ruby a psychopathic lover of policemen also on his own—a random association of two loonies. It is lunatics who are the real menace to crowned heads.) The next reaction was touching. Everybody in Texas, where the murder took place, everybody in New Orleans, where the murderer was born, began to feel personally guilty. A good deal of hatred toward Kennedy had been developing in the South, a) because he came from the North and the Civil War has never been forgotten, b) because he was antisegregation and perhaps c) because it was felt that he had bungled the Cuban situation. The consciousness of this hatred, though it had never been even near the level of assassination, made the Southerners blush with shame. Everybody felt, especially when the second killing took place, that the watching world would think ill of Americans. It was like a schoolboy's innocent guilt, very affecting.

Americans are a people who, like the Irish, have not had the benefit of spending a couple of hundred years under the discipline of the Lex and Pax Romana—the education of S.P.Q.R. They are not English, but then they are not French or Italian or Mexican or Negro either. They are all these, in the intensely important process of fusion, and the future, if there is a future, is certain to come from them. This is at present the most exciting place on earth.

Americans have a streak of lawlessness. In 1961, one murder happened every hour—this in a population of about 190 million. Somebody said on the radio yesterday, "There is a strain of violence in U. S. nature." It is to be expected. In the first place, they are bred from parents who had enough individualism, anarchy, guts, or whatever you like to call it, to emigrate. They are not bred from stay-at-homes. They are bred from the rebels who burst out. In the second place, in spreading over the relentless continent and winning the West, they have had to establish law as they pushed forward their boundaries by the individual law of the gun. In the third place, as I have been telling my audiences for two months, they are living in an actual Renaissance, a new birth of culture. People who live in Renaissances are apt to live with violence—like Marlowe or Webster or Ford. Here and now, with the cops and the gangsters and the outrages which suddenly explode, we are among the Borgias again and know the Duchess of Malfi.

Americans are young, inexperienced, idealistic, sentimental, longing for culture, confiding, lovable, wanting to be loved. They are as sweet in this way as boys at puberty, as touching, as protectable. They long to be grown-up, "correct."

After killing their President, they looked upon me uncertainly, blushing, guilty, fearing *and hoping* that I would scold them for doing wrong.

It was a deep shock to them. The people of Dallas are going about saying doubtfully, We are not really wicked?

This voluntary acceptance of blame, this innocent ambition to be an adult civilization, moved me very much.

Fortunately, in the sunlight of the late fall, it was a perfect funeral. There were no visible journalists, no crowding, no need for policemen, no vulgarity, no hysteria. Thousands upon thousands of people conducted themselves with silent dignity, sorrow and reflection in a wonderful, daylong purgation of emotion which brought the act of horror under control again.

Kennedy's death will probably do more good for the cause of integration than his life.

I watched the four-day serial on a beat-up TV set in the hospital. It was odd to see the dead President's demagogic cares being shifted from his simple and restful grave to the shoulders of his successor.

Well, death may be what life is for.

27 · 11 · 63

Adolescent America. Of course I am writing of the average, not of the intellectual—who is as international as anybody else. The average person is simple, religious, modest if not Puritan about sex, proud of his nation and particularly of his own birthplace, uncultured but respectful to culture, anxious as any other adolescent to be admired for being right, essentially good, benevolent, sentimental, prone like the young to outbursts, not very intelligent, dedicated to the herd, obtuse about variants, vigorous, in short like most other average schoolboys. He has a hard side of obstinate intolerance which comes out in witch hunts—most adolescents want to "belong" to clubs or societies—Ku Klux Klans—and he is uncertain about the difference between right and wrong, uncertain whether he is being "correct." The American dreams of ancientry and pedigree, as schoolboys dream of having been the sons of kings. His charm is that he *wants* to be good—surely it is better to be a do-gooder than a do-badder—and that he is trying with the truthful idealism of a nice teenager to become a great man.

He most certainly will, and I love him.

I have been reading about New Orleans, even if I can't explore it. (The collapse was exhaustion. My mind and body suddenly struck work, psychosomatically, fixing on the weakest link, the gall bladder. I walked about in agony all one night, reluctant to wake the Unkaufs, and was trundled off to the hospital in the morning, canceling four lectures. It was that or death.) New Orleans has one central feature, its ironwork. This is not an ancient feature. The town was originally French (1717), then Spanish, then resumed by Napoleon, then sold to Jefferson under the Louisiana Purchase. In 1788 it was destroyed by fire, all traces of the original wooden houses of the adventurers being swept away. It must have been rebuilt in a Spanish classical style with a certain amount of wooden or wrought-iron railing here and there, but it was not till the *1870's* that the astonishing cast-iron frills were added which are now its main charm. Its greatest rarity is a couple of fantastic iron fences modeled on Indian corn (sweet corn) with the cobs painted—very massive, intricate, lush and elegant.

The city is within touching distance of a great selection of cultures—it can touch Spanish river pirates (I bought a doubloon) and royal French bastards and an English army defeated by General Jackson and quadroon mistresses and tortured slaves and Catholic priests and voodoo under a famous voodoo queen called Marie Laveau and flatboat Yankees and palatial river boats, full of sparks and gamblers and bare-shouldered *villes*, and Harriet Martineau and Mark Twain, God bless him, and Bourbon Street where the prostitutes parade, and Dixie which perhaps takes its name from a Louisiana bank note called a "dix," and streets named Good Children, Love, Madman's, Mystery, Piety, Pleasure, Virtue and Desire. New Orleans was the city of *A Streetcar Named Desire.*

28 · 11 · 63

Thanksgiving.

Three hundred and forty-two years ago the Pilgrims who had fled to America from Europe, just as Brigham Young fled to the Salt Lake from Illinois, gathered their first harvest of sweet corn, etc. Their life had depended on it, their continuance on this continent. They held a Thanksgiving Service, which has been celebrated ever since.

I used to think that this version of the English Harvest Festival was a piece of sentimentality. Now that I know a little more about being a pioneer, now that I remember the story of those potatoes which the Mormons had to plant before they broke their fast, now that I can imagine the minute fingerhold by which the Pilgrim Fathers clung to the cliff-face of this tremendous continent—half of them died the first winter—I think it is a glorious thing to celebrate.

It is as important to Americans as, say, Easter Bank Holiday is to the cockney, and they eat turkey on this day and give each other presents. One old gentleman in the hospital got six candies in a cardboard wigwam from the 5th Grade of Audubon School, and wrote to thank them.

This about young America joining gangs. The average American is clubable. He likes to belong. He will join anything from the Elks to the Shriners to the K.K.K. to the Comus crew to the college fraternities with Greek letters like ØBK to the Boston Club here in New Orleans—which was haughty enough to exclude Governor Long. (Jews cannot belong to Comus, far less Negroes.) For that matter, his *religions* are something to belong to—from Catholic to Latter-day Saints. I think this is a good thing. The religions are alive and active and they give a discipline, a continuum, a bannister, a tramline to guide the young—a discipline whose lack in Britain has produced the poor Beatnik. It is easier to be a tram than a bus. It helps the young to start them off on rails, even if they become automobiles later.

But secret societies can be dangerous. When I was about ten years old at my private school, I belonged to a club called The Black Hand. We wore cardboard badges in the reverse of our buttonholes with a sort of Hand of Ulster drawn on them—I seem to remember some drops of blood in red ink—but did not know what else we existed for. Eventually we held some sort of trial, condemned the lowest in our pecking order to be beaten, and did beat him till I managed to stop it, suddenly realizing it was real.

This sort of thing *could* happen to the Puritanism of America. God help us if the organized club which America is, a sort of non-secret society, ever gets it into its head that its communal secret is being menaced by another club. Salem witch hunts, McCarthyism, John Birch Societies, and Un-American Activities Committees are manifestations of this tendency. If the whole nation gets good cause to believe that its Puritan plutocracy is really being attacked by Communism, it will react with shattering, self-righteous, convinced ferocity. Somebody ought to explain to Khrushchev about this. If he pushes this club-joining adolescence too far, it will react with terrible, juvenile, pitiless violence. The Ku Klux Klan won't be in it.

Meanwhile, when Episcopalian or any other clergy come to pray over me in hospital, I accept their prayers with gratitude and affection, because the prayers are a mode of kindness.

I suppose I am condescending to the Americans again, writing about their adolescence, because of the truly ghastly pap and crap which I get on TV all day, as I lie here alone. Judging by the TV only, the mental age of the U. S. would be about minus ten.

It is important to remember that such a level of culture does exist, alongside the college cultures I have been visiting, and that it is among our greatest dangers.

29 · 11 · 63

After having nothing to eat for 24 hours, nothing to drink for 12, thirteen pills at five-minute intervals, 3 enemas, one blood test, two cardiograms and two X-rays, I have little to report about the American scene today except the cheering news, to air travelers like ourselves, that a DC-8 with 118 passengers has crashed in Canada without survivors. A two-engined Cessna went into the lake here the day before yesterday, killing her five passengers.

30 · 11 · 63

Well, Carol has had a fortnight on the tiles with the family of her kind godparents and seems to be refreshed.

1 · 12 · 63

I was in the hospital yesterday and at about six o'clock tonight we are on our travels again.

The moon is at one night after the full and we have a DC-8, rather an old one. We rule our way above a gleaming, muddy, channeled plain of sea or mudflat in the silver light, and then there are the lighted towns like heaps of pearls and phosphorescent amoebae on the nightlit ocean-floor of earth over which we are the metal fish. At first there is an underpopulated nightscape sometimes almost all dark, then cloud under us while we eat a four-course meal at thirty-three thousand feet, then again we are over the jewelry of several spaced-out cities rather like those thin starfish which have an extra number of legs, spider webs of light, cobwebs of it, protozoa on the deeper darkness of our sea floor—then an empty country with single lights as rare and scattered as the few stars above them, more cloud, finally in the distance the long, luminous blur of Washington with its dead President laid still under his little butane lamp. A yawn renews the rumble of our jets, I stub out my cigarette and fasten the seat belt. We have covered 966 miles.

Dulles Airport is remarkable for the number of its blue lights—a sort of endless military cemetery of them.

The temperature must have been around 70° in New Orleans. Here it is 28°.

Our long taxi drive takes us past Arlington Cemetery, where we crane back through the rear window to look with sorrow and respect toward the single spark of Kennedy's grave.

2 · 12 · 63

The talk to the Library of Congress was not unsuccessful. We had luncheon with members of its staff in the Whittall Pavilion, presided over by the Librarian of Congress, after which Carol went off to visit the President's grave and I rested a bit at the hotel, going over my talk about Georgian Poets. The lecture was at 8:30 in the Coolidge Auditorium (seating 511) and was recorded—by kind permission of Colston Leigh!

The Library of Congress has about thirteen million books and pamphlets. It was originally burned by the British and refounded on the basis of our dear Jefferson's personal collection.

After the lecture I kissed hands with Mrs. Whittall, aged ninety-six, who is the benefactor of this branch of culture here and who bought the A. E. Housman Mss. as a present for the library. She was pleased that much of the talk had been about Housman.

The Library is an Imperial Corinthian marble affair built in 1897, and its reading room is round, like the one at the British Museum where I used to be so happy as a young scholar.

3 · 12 · 63

We spent the morning shopping for Xmas presents for Europe and went by taxi to the Library of Congress again, to see if we could get a postcard of the building. As the taxi flashed past the main entrance we *thought* we saw a bronze group of Tritons or people of that sort, perhaps in a fountain, whose central figure seemed not to be wearing a fig leaf. The taxi was moving fast and I am old and wear spectacles and the group was on the opposite side of the vehicle to me. But if this is so, it is the first entire male statue we have seen in a public place during our vast expedition around the United States.

The cabdriver told us that Washington owes its splendid lighting of its public buildings to Queen Elizabeth of Britain. It seems that when she came here even Lincoln's colossal seated figure in his monument was hardly visible at night, and she commented on this, and since then the wonderful public buildings and memorials of their city have been beautifully, or at least more beautifully, illuminated. It gave me a glow to hope this was true.

We left Washington by the Pennsylvania Railroad through the wintry woods and past the gray small wooden homesteads that border Chesapeake Bay. We crossed three times the wind-streaked waters which were its tributaries. There were flocks of duck on one of them, which I took to be buffleheads. I fetched a P.R. matchbox from the club car for Carol. She is making a collection of these flat, cardboard match cases. We arrived at Wilmington in the dark—say 80 miles—and were met by the happy and friendly chaplain of St. Andrew's School, Middletown, the Rev. Edward Gammons. He drove us at once to the school, about 25 miles, after dropping our bags at the Du Pont Hotel in Wilmington.

It is difficult to keep your head and write soberly about emotional exchanges. You tend to love people who love you, perhaps blindly. Anyway, the boys kept me on the platform from 7:30 till 9 P.M., when I was forcibly removed from their heartwarming goodness and kindness and affection and intelligence. This is the second time in my life, and will doubtless be the last, when I have won a standing ovation —not won, but been given it—and the charming, happy, obviously loved headmaster told Carol that it had never happened before at St. Andrews. It is eerie, deeply moving, almost frightening, when a big theatre rises at you in a storm of clapping, first two, then five, then twelve, then all, overwhelming you with a sort of murder of kindness, as if they were going to tear you to bits.

There was nothing I could do except bow, and feel like tears, and write the name of the place on my heart. I have after all struggled a long way across the United States, trying to give to the audiences, and this pays for all, once and for all and fully.

St. Andrew's School is not state supported, it is a private enterprise much like an English Public School of the best kind, endowed by Alexis Du Pont through his own munificence in 1929 (what a memorial!) and devoted to boys of fourteen to nineteen who pay about two thousand dollars a year. The ratio of masters to boys is one to seven. It is not coeducational. The children row on the Delaware (fours), wrestle as their favorite speciality, do not beat each other or get beaten by their teachers, keep the splendid buildings clean with their own hands on a "job system" which works out at about 30 minutes daily of housework for every boy who is not in the sixth form. I may have been deceived by my emotions of gratitude, but they struck me as being singularly happy and decent people, and one of the things that pleased me most was at the faculty reception afterwards. The headmaster, Mr. Robert Moss, obviously an angel who lives in the same circle of supermen as the late J. F. Roxburgh of Stowe, had noticed every boy who asked a question, and was reflecting about that boy's character, and why he asked it, and was pleased and proud when perhaps a shy boy had spoken.

The whole place is run *on a bluff*. If you love people, and are good, you can bluff them into loving you back in a wonderful way. These children had been beautifully kidded into an honor system based on one simple proposition: "If you agree to enter this school, you are on your honor to accept certain restrictions. If you do not want to be on your honor in this respect, you are at liberty to go away." But they were not solemn and goody-goody about it. If you poured in or cut your name on your desk, you were asked to sandpaper it off. If you wrote dirty words on the wall (which happened last week) the whole school got fined 15 cents per boy. But I got an absolute roar of applause by urging everybody to write *everywhere* on *all* the walls, thus bankrupting the entire institution at a blow. In fact, they were not solemn about their goodness.

This is one of the places I shall remember always.

The headmaster had the visible features of goodness. Apart from his pleased and humorous face, he had an enormous black Newfoundland bitch called Chloe who did not have to inhabit a dog kennel (this is one of the things the Americans are bad about) but obviously owned the house and lay on most of it, sighing with benevolence.

At the Boston ovation, I was on a stage above the audience so they had to stand and clap upwards at me. Here, my reading desk was on the floor of a slanting auditorium so that the audience was higher than I was. They towered over and crushed me with enthusiasm as they stood. They were like a wave.

We have visited a great many schools and colleges and universities now, and I am certain in my own mind that coeducation is not a blessing until you reach university age, if then.

After all, you are at school to be educated, not to make love, and there is a suitable age for everything. The schools where the sexes were celibate have one and all been brighter—had more steam up—than the ones where half the learning time, or much more than half, was devoted to the boy friend or the girl friend. University level is young enough, if not too young, for coeducation. Williams College, our very first, was an unforgotten case in point. However bitterly the youths complained of lack of females, they did have the weekends for that object, and during the week they were simply teeming with creative activities, in theatre or movies or anything else. This was at University level. At some of the coeducational colleges we have visited, the young people seemed to sit back hand in hand, waiting for the faculty to lay on the entertainment and to serve the cocktails.

The great American Renaissance of culture which we have been witnessing, its vast outpouring of riches upon knowledge, seems to me to be best served at places like St. Andrew's and Marymount and Williams College. And we have noticed that discipline pays. Our best coeducational establishments, at University level, have been run by the tight creeds of Jesuits or Mormons or Wesleyans. I shall always love and remember most of all Boston and Salt Lake City and Middletown, Delaware, and Ohio Wesleyan. And I feel ashamed, too, to single out these in such an arbitrary way, where practically all have been charming.

It is sad and presumably the mark of being an old man to end up with such conservative, such Tory, conclusions. But the conclusions are based on a wide sample. Our brightest institutions have been those with discipline, and often those with celibacy.

Somebody mentioned during the faculty party that our highest figure of unmarried mothers in coeducational establishments (4 percent) was not high enough. He said he would place it nearer 6 percent. He himself had been at Harvard.

I wrote to the headmaster, inviting him and his wife and Chloe and any or all of the boys to come and stay with me in Alderney. They have promised me a pennant of the school. I have written to my publishers to send their library bound copies of all my books, but I must get hold of them and sign them first.

Now we must brace ourselves for a hard week. After tomorrow's evening lecture we actually catch a train at about 11 P.M., reach our destination after midnight, and must catch another train by 7 A.M., and lecture twice that day. I have tottered out of the hospital into this sort of thing, but places like St. Andrew's make anything worth while. Anything.

6 · 12 · 63

This is Friday the 6th, and we are in New York, and I have to sum up as best I can the struggles of the last three days.

Wilmington, Delaware, was where the journal left off—a place which has a good deal to do with past history. You remember, there, the not too ancient times when America belonged to nobody but the Indians, when European nations were competing to occupy the New World. The Swedes were the first successful colony in Delaware (a Dutch colony had been massacred to a man) and under them the town of Wilmington was called Fort Christina. They in turn got dispossessed again by the Dutch of New Amsterdam (now New York) and finally the English—who had settlements north and south—took over. So it was worth looking over the little museum in the old Court House, which we did.

We lectured successfully to a thing called The Hadley Fund at the Unionville High School in Kennett Square, Pennsylvania, in the evening, and were brought back to Wilmington afterwards. Say it was 20 miles each way.

The Hadley Fund was an interesting institution, typical of this American cultural renaissance which we have been visiting. A Mr. and Mrs. Hadley had left a sum of money not to any college or art gallery but to their own small community at Kennett Square, suggesting only that it should be spent on culture. Mr. Hadley had also suggested that the principal should be invested in oil. So here was a town with something like $400,000 to spend (if I remember the figure correctly) and they were happily blowing part of it on me. The people were charming, the lecture was successful, and there we were back in Wilmington after dark. We were in time to catch a train for Philadelphia, which got us there past midnight.

Conversation in train: "We only ever," observed Carol, "arrive at Philadelphia at dead of night and leave at crack of dawn." "Yes, it's sad. They signed the Declaration of Independence here too, and I believe they have the Liberty Bell."

So we stumbled bleary-eyed into bed and crawled out again reeling at 6 A.M., to catch the most miserable train in the world at the most miserable station (North Broad Street,

Philadelphia, may it shortly fall to bits). Oh, the misery before dawn—the dirty, cold waiting room full of darkies and the feeble heaters high in the roof for fear we wreck them and wire netting in the dusty glass windows in case we all went mad and smashed them to bits, and no coffee or any food obtainable to break our fast, neither in that morgue nor in the train we were waiting for. It was dirtier and more wretched than any London suburban station on a lost branch line on strike. There was a strange, grimy iron fence down the middle of the tracks, presumably to prevent us from committing suicide. Nobody even knew which platform the train would be coming to, and there were 1½ hours in front of us with empty stomachs. Oh God! Oh, Philadelphia! And, just to brighten up the joint that icy morning, they had dyed the train windows green.

We chugged the 56 miles to Reading, Pennsylvania, past black wintry trees and dingy pools and canals and drear wooden dollhouses in disrepair and a still, gray river called the Schuylkill, through a version of the English Midlands with mean streams full of thrown-away motor tires, with a colored man on the seat behind us hawking and sneezing with a cold. The only diversion was the horn and bell of our engine at level crossings, always pleasantly railwaylike and faintly reminiscent of cow-catchers.

We got some breakfast at a diner in Reading, then took a taxi to Albright College where I was to lecture at 11:10 A.M.

The lecture was a success (in the chapel) and as usual everybody was charming. The uglier a place is the more the inhabitants seem to long for you to admire it and, after the school lunch, we were taken by car up a small mountain to view the foggy red roofs of this once prosperous railway terminus. A very nice and hopeful boy came with the Librarian and a friend to show us over. He had an 8 m.m. camera with no exposure meter, and I longed for his future success in TV and felt myself to be a pig for not admiring very much the hometown which they displayed for us with tender patriotism. They kept saying how beautiful it would be in the spring—indeed, perhaps it is beautiful and we were too tired to appreciate it. There was a Chinese pagoda on the hill from which we viewed the little town and aspiring college, and certainly we were able to wish them well. They brought us back to the station with loving kindness, and stayed to wave until the train went out.

Conversation in train as I photograph a grim barn out of the green window: Me: "I just want it as a memento of this dreadful journey." Carol: "I think I'll take a blank picture."

A curiosity at Reading was a statue of an elk which had spikes on its back to prevent children sitting on it.

Three Amish in black hats and beards were in our carriage, talking exclusively among themselves.

We got back to Philadelphia in time for the traffic rush hour, finally found a taxi which would accept us, crawled into the hotel at 5:10 P.M.—to find a note saying that the sponsors of the next lecture would collect us at 5:15!

We dined—that's still Thursday the 5th—with rather a grand party at the famous ladies' college of Bryn Mawr, before lecturing to the Main Line School Night Association at 8 P.M., my second lecture of the long day. It was again successful—a most beautiful and almost brand-new theatre for the high school of this rich neighborhood of Rosenmont,

Pennsylvania. The audience was about 1,100, and the one in the morning was about 600, but I have rather given up counting heads since the 12,000 in Utah.

The Main Line Association is another facet of the American cultural drive. This time it was a self-supporting, non-profit-making association of local subscribers who offered, apart from lectures, an abundance of training courses—including one in dry-fly fishing!

Mrs. Bunting and Mr. Riely drove us happily back to the hotel, where we fell into bed before midnight.

I felt bad about having been poor company at dinner, in saving up my failing energies for the platform, and I also feel ashamed of writing unsympathetically about Reading and Philadelphia, when our schedule never gave them a chance. The student at Albright College, who was proud of the place and proud to be with us and in every way full of simplicity and hope and goodwill, was called Ed Bunn.

Everybody at Wilmington had been hospitably delighted to inform us that the British won the local battle of Brandywine in 1777.

So now, on the 6th, we are back by train in New York—another 70 miles or so—and I have had my publisher to luncheon and had a meeting with my literary agent and been shopping with Carol on Fifth Avenue.

The public statues in New York are so shy that they won't even settle for tin towels. Atlas seems to have draped himself in a motor tire.

It now appears that one of President Kennedy's favorite discs was the cast recording of *Camelot.* It is an odd coincidence, because I have been told that when King George VI of England died, my book called *The Goshawk* was found on his bed.

Anyway, my life is practically composed of coincidences. Why should there be another living writer called T. H. White, and why should he have been chosen by the Book of the Month Club the very next month after I was chosen?

7 · 12 · 63

Today we are off by train to the Emma Willard School at Troy, New York. It is that lovely journey up the Hudson which we have made before, and I hope to get a chance of photographing Bannerman's Island Arsenal. In the evening, and for the weekend, we shall be staying with the poet William Jay Smith—blessed be God—and his poetess wife, Barbara Howes.

The Emma Willard School was founded by a feminist born in 1787. She memorialized the New York State Legislature in 1819 on the subject of women's education and seems to have started the school around about then. . . .

9 · 12 · 63

How am I to write about our minor triumph at Emma Willard and the happy weekend, of which we still have a few hours left, staying with the two poets at their farmhouse in the snows and bare woods of Vermont? I always thought

I was better at charming boys than girls, so it was a happy surprise when I was given yet another standing ovation by the kind, pretty and intelligent girls thirteen to eighteen of this expensive and comparatively ancient boarding school. We have found everywhere that teaching establishments have brighter scholars when the sexes are separated and when there is discipline from the faculty (any belief, from Catholicism to Mormonism will do.) Now we have to add a further observation. On the whole, the more expensive schools are the brighter ones—perhaps because of the proportion of teachers to pupils. At Emma Willard, if you leave out the physical education staff, etc., the proportion seems to be about one to fourteen. The accurate (but dead) Gothic architecture is a bit like that of Boston College and is bound to have a civilizing effect on people who inhabit it, the faculty is devoted to the pupils, and the general lines on which the place in run are not unlike the system at St. Andrew's. One excellent feature of the curriculum is that all the arts and sciences are taken in a historical sequence—you start off as a sophomore with those of Greece or Rome, move to the Middle Ages, etc., as a junior and end up as a senior with the culture of present times. There was snow on the beautiful campus and a lighted Christmas tree and everybody was preparing for their annual pageant called the Revels—an affair in which the seniors dress in Elizabethan costumes for a sort of Yuletide banquet with beefeaters and Morris dances and a morality play (St. George and the Dragon and the Turk and the Doctor)....

13 · 12 · 63

So it is Friday the 13th of December, and we are back again in New York, and I have a day to spare in which to make some feeble effort to write up the past week. Our tour has been ending in a blaze of happiness, and I am miserable that it will soon be over, and more and more things have been becoming obvious.

In the first place, I never ought to have visited clubs or commercial forums or perhaps even universities. Our ceiling ought to have been colleges, in spite of the grand reception I got at Provo and elsewhere. What place does Merlin have talking to grown-ups? They are past listening. All my life I have got on better with children and adolescents, found them more receptive, affectionate and grateful for truth. They ask better questions, consider your answers more seriously, and are at closer, vivider, more intimate grips with life.

A second thing is about my kind and efficient Carol. Her whole family told us we would quarrel before we started, and, in the arduous, exhausting, three months' journey, we have sometimes hated each other's guts. But we have never spoken all the wounding words we might have spoken, we have carried on with a tenacious loyalty to our bargain in the face of quite a lot of strain—for instance, we left New Hampton yesterday at 2 P.M. in a blizzard and did not get to New York, by a terrible train, till after midnight—this after I had taken three classes in the morning, rising at 8 A.M. We have weathered an experience which perhaps few girls of eighteen have faced. We can be silent together when we are tired, because we trust each other. There is a link between us of achievement and, on my side, of admiration which can never be altered now.

Without her, I would have missed all my connections, lost all my baggage, and incidentally I would have been dead. We are already planning another journey in which she will be the agent as well as the secretary, and if this isn't Sucks and Boo to the pessimists at the beginning, I don't know what is.

To get back to Emma Willard last Saturday.

It is the same sort of school as Carol went to herself (Queenswood) and in fact it exchanges scholars with that institution. Its basic fee is $3,000 a year. The girls were bright, intelligent and keen without, thank God, being manly, and the whole place had an atmosphere of happiness which was to be shared by our next two campuses.

I was assured, with exasperation, at Union College, that Emma Willard is surrounded by an electrified fence to exclude male visitors! It would be nice to believe this, but difficult, though I have no doubt that male visitors would like to be there.

They and the faculty kept us talking till after midnight, when Bill Smith turned up in a snowstorm to drive us the thirty miles back to his home in Vermont. Americans seem to drive at least fifty miles a day without turning a hair. They have to. They inhabit a continent, not an island like us, and for them Rome would be a neighbor to London.

We had a weekend of freedom before us, in an American

home, the home moreover of two cultivated poets who had sons to make it homely and two dogs to enjoy the freedom thereof and a sort of science-fiction door, which would have delighted the heart of Sir Isaac Newton, by which the dogs could push their way in and out. For the next two days we went to local parties or lolled about in the comfortable, wooden, snowbound farmhouse of the Smiths, arguing about architecture and poetry and politics and Harold Acton (a mutual friend four thousand miles away) and Paris and Florence and India and the economic collapse of England because India was doing its own plumbing and Huey Long and an Ode to the Telephone (Ring on, ring on, I'm on the john) and saving dogs which have been abandoned by their owners (which is what Barbara Howes takes the trouble to do) and son Greg's ambitions and abilities and about a scheme for designing an American type-face based on Benjamin Franklin's or else on the "wanted" notice and newspapers of the forty-niners. I thought that Williams College ought to have such a printing machine and should print the best of its own literature.

Bill, who is a politician as well as a poet—incidentally talking perfect French with a Parisian accent and pretty good Italian as well—teased me by insisting that the liquor consumption in Utah is the highest in the U. S.

It was snowy and it was Vermont—by the way, we were in the Green Mountains and that, it suddenly dawned on me, was the meaning of Vert-Mont. We visited Williams College again, where we had been kindly received so long ago, and we bought from the town's magnificent bookshop (Williams' Bookstore) a quantity of books to be sent to

Alderney. The proprietor made me a present of two censorable works and would accept no payment for them. We also visited Bennington, the free-and-easy and famous college for girls—at which it is said that there are only two rules. You must wear shoes at least in the dining hall and if you won't be in before 6 A.M. you must ring up. It is also said that some students of Williams College are reluctant to visit Bennington for fear of being captured and never seen again. These libels are relished by the real inhabitants.

We went too to view the superb interior of Bennington Church, and the lovely graveyard where Robert Frost is buried, and to the battlefield's monument where the British lost yet another battle. We have become impervious to this and don't mind any longer who won.

I saw the woven nest of an oriole hanging from a tree over the icy road.

Americans, we decided after arguing with the neighbors, are essentially an *earnest* people. They have so much love and kindness and are so little blasé. But it is fatal to forget that they are all descended from *people who had the guts not to stay at home.* Americans are not English or Irish or Italian or anything else. They are the children, in a melting pot, of adventurers who had this one thing in common, that they were individualists who had the courage, initiative and vigor to break out of the Old World and conquer a continent. These joiners, like the joiners of that club at my private school, have joined the club of America. If somebody strikes against it, as happened at Pearl Harbor, they will always react with a blind, devastating energy. Americans are more likely to let off an atomic bomb than the Russians are. They are less old, less effete with history, more bred from strength, younger, more lovable, more terrible potentially.

Well, the weekend was over too soon and a pleasant student of Williams College, by the name of Phil Walters, drove us down the snowy mountains to Schenectady, where I was to lecture at Union College. This college was founded as such in 1795 and had educated the father of Franklin D. Roosevelt and the grandfather of Winston Churchill. It was as splendid as it ought to be with such a tradition, and as happy and intelligent as any we had visited. Its endowment had risen from nought to about $26,000,000, its enrollment to a grand total of 1,976 in 1962, and its basic fees are about $2,950 a year. Its tendency is toward science and engineering. It is expanding like all the other educational establishments we have visited on this tour of the American cultural renaissance. Unfortunately, to make way for a new library which may or may not be magnificent, they are at present pulling down a beautiful piece of Victorian red brick architecture (Washburn Hall) and, if somebody doesn't raise a stink, they may even have the folly to destroy the Nott Memorial Library, which is as individual an example of American Victorian as any in the States.

I lectured in the chapel at 11:30 A.M., lunched with the students and Dr. Kilburn, and argued with all and sundry about every subject under the sun until nightfall, in the hall of the students' center. We enjoyed ourselves very much.

I have probably survived this trip as well or better than Carol (who was writing letters, poor dear) because I manage to draw energy, youth, affection and encouragement from the charmers I talk to and who offer these refreshments so freely and generously.

Youth is more honest than old age as well as being more beautiful.

One of the bright ideas suddenly produced by a student while we were arguing about discipline and coercion in low-grade New York schools where the semidelinquent pupils actually don't want to be educated was this. "We get called up for National Service" he said. "Now that we have push-button warfare, why not abolish the Army and call up millions of students to be teachers instead?"

Finally we were driven to Albany airport in the dark, where we plodded across the icy tarmac, the snow-spume riffling against our ankles, to board an elderly Convair belonging to Mohawk Airlines. We were cheered by the fact that another 707 had just been obliterated near Wilmington, Delaware, where we were last week.

It was bumpy and we just sat in the semigloom with seat belts fastened, too tired even to read, while a lightless America jerked about below us until we reached the smoother air of the coastal plain. Then there were the lighted Chinese dragons—the great embroidered mantle of lights—of the Boston coast. Then there was a taxi. Then, at about 8:45, there were Father Sweeney and Father Shea waiting for us in the foyer of the Somerset Hotel, where we had invited them to dinner and a bottle of wine. We were alumni, by now, of Boston College—where we got our first heart-warming experience of a standing ovation—and we had come back, as was only right and proper, to report to the fathers the progress of our tour.

All this last part, including the trip to Williams College,

was a kind of little thanksgiving of our own—for we had no lecturing business in Boston—to acknowledge the joy and happiness and hospitality which we have been given for three months.

We won't forget Father Shea chanting ecclesiastically about the fisherman who had no truth in him (his own version of Handel, for he is an accomplished musician and writer of musical comedies) nor Father Sweeney going off with Carol to sing sentimental Irish songs at the piano in the bar. We showed them what we had previously written about Boston College and Father Sweeney's first reaction was, "Oh, but *do* mention it was only a few malcontents who criticized our theology." Father Shea, reading the next paragraph where I had emphasized how good it is to find teachers who allow themselves to be criticized, said, "No. You are quite right. You have told the truth." I offered to cut out anything they pleased. They said, "No. We trust you. We are in your hands."

It was a wonderful reunion and, as usual, Father Shea had to be ticked off by Father Sweeney for using bad language.

They are both darlings and we sent our love by them to everybody at the college.

I have arranged for seven copies of each of my books to be bound in leather and sent to each of seven addresses. I shall have to come back to New York to sign them. I need not mention what one of the addresses is.

Now, after the usual late to bed and early to rise, it was 75 miles from Boston to Concord by the wintry, beautiful, cold, sunny, polluted waters of the Merrimac, between its hibernal trees. We were in a train with no restaurant car. At

Concord we were met by a station wagon with spikes on the roof to hold skis—as we have seen, the Americans have a passion for spikes in unlikely places—and driven about 32 miles to New Hampton through a countryside like the lowlands of Scotland.

The new Hampton School is for boys of about fourteen to eighteen, it was founded in 1821, skis and skates are desirable in the school outfit, and its basic fees are about $2,600. It is not half so well endowed as it ought to be and must be. I here and now urge any multimillionaire who may be able to read enough to decipher these lines to send to the headmaster, Mr. Thomas Holmes Moore, an ex-fighter pilot of the Navy, the sum of one billion dollars unconditionally.

Reasons why multimillionaires must increase the endowment of New Hampton:

Like so many schools, colleges and universities in the U. S., it runs its own radio station—but, unlike many, it is producing next January its own musical comedy called *A Man Among Men,* written, composed, acted and directed by its own students. It also has a well-known glee club, and Double Quartet.

It is a place of complete racial and religious tolerance, but it does accept a reasonable discipline which seems to depend on the fanatical energy and enthusiasm of the headmaster, whom the boys treat as a valued friend. (They knock cheerfully on the windows of his car as he drives among them and treat him with confidence when it is a matter of censoring the school magazines or theatrical productions.)

It produces a magazine called *Jabberwocky* from which, since I gave it three of my own poems, I take the liberty of transcribing a copy of verses by a writer signing himself Rax.

Tick

Father Time,
You unshaven wizened old man,
The reason you are not
Stopped and held (like
A newborn child) is that no one
Wants a perpetual miser.
What good
Has saving done you?
We laugh at your creeping ways
And point at the ludicrous hour-glass;
Using it to measure three-minute eggs.
Nor can you speak our language
But must dabble in ticks and tocks,
In snicks and clicks.
Your inexpressive circling
Gestures impress not a soul.

Silly old man,
Go trip on your scythe.

Its students not only kept me arguing half the night and most of the next morning—and arguing about everything from fig leaves on statues to whether to give America's surplus grain to China—but they also, while I was there, won the basketball matches of both their teams. We watched one game, and the intelligent boys were good physical specimens.

It is a family. There are about 250 boys in it. They seem to be on friendly terms with each other, conversing freely at meals. Their standard of music and painting is high. They are generous, and two separate pupils presented me with books to improve my mind. Another one drew and gave me a portrait of myself.

I invited the headmaster and his wife and five children and dog, as well as half the students, to come and stay in Alderney.

These few reasons, though there are many more, seem to be enough for presenting them with such a small matter as a billion dollars.

By the way, by their own efforts they have doubled their numbers since 1954 and put up two new buildings this year, but the future emphasis is likely to be on quality rather than quantity.

Well, we stayed the night in the headmaster's home—he drove me like the slavedriver he is, for the boys' benefit—not at all against my inclinations—and Carol wrote some of our endless mail and the snow became a small blizzard. The night temperature had been 12°. All aircraft were grounded in that part of the East Coast. So our travel plans had to be changed.

The station wagon took us slowly over the ice-sheathed roads to White River Junction in an hour and a half, leaving the school with much regret at about 2 P.M. At White River Junction we caught a slow train to New York (no diner) and arrived in this city, at ten minutes past midnight, still wearing the headmaster's overshoes, after eight and a half mortal hours in that terrible railway carriage. I estimate the distance to be less than 250 miles. It was not so much our very moderate speed as the countless stops and endless waits at them.

Even then we had trouble in getting a taxi. I fell into bed

around 1 A.M., not pausing to work out the following mileage of our arduous six days:

New York to Albany	say 150	miles
Albany to Emma Willard	10	
E.W. to the Smiths'	30	
Smiths' to Schenectady	45	
Schenectady to Albany	10	
Albany via Springfield to Boston	150	
Boston to Concord	75	
Concord to New Hampton	32	
New Hampton to White River Junction	45	
White River to New York	250	
	797	miles

All these distances are a guess. It was agony. It was worth it.

Conversation in a train, as Carol stares drearily at a ticket which has N.Y., N.H., & H.R.R. printed on it:

"What can that last H stand for?"

"Hell."

14 · 12 · 63

Last night Carol went off to dine with some friend or relation—she is a great homebody—so I took myself alone to see Albee's *Who's Afraid of Virginia Woolf?* The dialogue was brilliant, the exposition as professional as Ibsen's and the while thing splendid "theatre." The situation is a little slight for serious drama. In fact it is a situation (inventing an imaginary son) which I dealt with myself several years ago in a short story for the *Evening Standard.* Still, it's an excellent and witty and polished piece of work. The movement of the actors around the stage, in a piece which was entirely conversational, was cleverly managed. The audience, who had been informed it was a comedy, laughed obediently in the wrong places.

Dialogue overheard on the stairs as we filed out:

She: "What did you think of it?"

He: "Well, it would be interesting to see it twice."

She: "What, the play?"

I got to the theatre nearly an hour too early and passed the time in rather a dubious bar nearby (coffee for me) whose clients were mostly colored people, some not very sober. But they accepted me without comment—which was polite of them, considering I have a white beard like rather a pettish Santa Claus and was wearing a Sherlock Holmes ulster and carrying a silver-mounted walking stick which had belonged to a classman of West Point in 1899. Two shady characters accosted me on the street but were content to be politely brushed off, and the cabdriver on the way home cross-examined me about Lawrence of Arabia. It was Friday the 13th and two of his children were ill on that account. However, I survived till midnight.

Somewhere or other last week, I think at Schenectady, we had a longish interview on TV to add to the general struggle. They promised to send a copy to Alderney.

Looking back over the long trek, I think the most impressive country thing of all to an Englishman is that nearly all

American houses are painted white or sometimes a splendid Indian red or, rarely, a good battleship gray. Other colors are more seldom seen and of course most houses are wooden and the paint is generally fresh and clean.

Today we went to see the English movie *Tom Jones.* Perhaps we had been looking forward to it too much, or perhaps I am spoiled by having gone to so many Italian movies last winter in Italy, but it was rather a disappointment. It did get better as it went along, and Hugh Griffith was as splendid as ever, but somehow it was too self-conscious— actors ought not to acknowledge the presence of the camera—too much done by theatre actors rather than cinema ones, and in some way not true to what I feel about the eighteenth century. Anyway it was below the standards of France and Italy.

Carol shopped with friends during the afternoon and evening. I stayed in the hotel and read Updike's *Rabbit, Run.*

15 · 12 · 63

We spend the morning tidying up a mass of correspondence, reading past press clippings and trying to see a little into the future. We have had no future for a long time, except the next airplane or train. Tomorrow is our last engagement, in Philadelphia—and, as usual, we have no chance to see the place, even on a third visit. It's a fatality.

At luncheon the waitress, an Irishwoman, said, "Did ye ever see de way dese peoples is going on? Dere was a boy kilt last night up where I am staying." "What color?" "He was white." "Was it a gang war?" "Yes, up in de Bronx." We have been seeing a section of the U. S. which is not fully representative—the educated section.

This hotel, by the way, the Roger Smith on Lexington Avenue, is still the best we have found in the U. S.—for being central, comfortable, hospitable, well fed and surprisingly cheap into the bargain.

We decided after lunch that it was disgraceful to abide in New York without going up the Empire State Building. I lived for about a year in the environs of Naples without getting to the top of Vesuvius, but now that I'm old I realize it was antisocial of me. So we went off with Carol's Aunt Molly and Cousin David to do our duty.

We craned up at the monstrous creature from street level with a kind of horror before we started. It is 1,472 feet high and is said to sway 20 feet or something. Snow and rain are sometimes seen falling upward, and the rain is sometimes red. You can see 80 miles at best—we had wonderful winter visibility—and its beacon can be seen from 300 miles away. Sixteen thousand people work in it—where once, in 1799, there stood the John Thompson farm. Our elevator reached the 80th floor in less than a minute, making me yawn as I do in a jet, and the building has 74 elevators whose speeds range from 600 to 1,200 ft. per minute—i.e., about 14 m.p.h vertically. Its marble comes from France, Italy, Belgium and Germany, exhausting whole quarries to match the blocks, and people who kiss each other at the high levels give each other electric shocks. It sells perfectly frightful souvenirs at the top.

I am ashamed to say I have lost my horror of height. Everything goes with age. I gave up being seasick when I was forty and now I can't even get a kick out of the Empire State Building.

Today's temperatures have been between 12° and 26°, but you don't feel it like in England. We have neither of us had a head cold since the trip started.

16 · 12 · 63

So in the end we have had the chance to see Philadelphia by daylight, crisp in the sunny winter snow. The students of La Salle College (Christian Brothers) gave me for the last time I shall get it the stunning applause and affection which makes my heart turn over, and I am miserable that the tour is finished, and I don't want to stop ever ever ever. How will I do now, without the generosity and enthusiasm of youth, and the hospitality of my beloved continent, and the excitement of airplanes and trains and cabs and automobiles and even ferry boats? We have not missed a single connection, except through being in the hospital, and we have gathered a sort of momentum of travel which does not know how to stop, and all the mountains, deserts, rivers, forests, homes, people, kindnesses, warmth, love, yes, love, novelty, discovery, beauty, grandeur, simplicity, seriousness, youth, vigor, enormousness of the United States combine to look over our shoulders and say, Don't go. I have become an *addict* to America—worse than alcohol. In spite of the killing struggle, perhaps because of it, I have never been happier in my life. In spite of the hospital—which was a psychosomatic worry about giving value for money, and was a repeat of the stomach attack which I had in this same hotel three months ago when worrying about the poetry I had to learn by heart—I have actually felt healthier and younger under the strain. How am I to do without it now, and how repay? I have been learning all the time, as I was constantly urging my audiences to learn, and it is an actual pang to stop, a pain in the heart not to know any longer that we must pack our drip-dries in the knapsacks on our shoulders and be off to Philadelphia in the morning.

La Salle College is in its centennial year—it was founded on March 20, 1863. In 1940 its enrollment was about 400—it is now nearly 5,000. It has no Medicean Grand Dukes (no millionaire benefactors) to support it, no benevolent cardinals to beg for it, and it is not state aided. By its own efforts alone and on a very low basic fee per resident student, approximately $1,600, it has built itself a $2 million Union Building in 1959 and a $2.5 million Science Center in 1960 and now it is after a new library for its centennial. I have been telling these boys all over the U. S. that they are living in the middle of a second cultural renaissance, and here it is with a vengeance.

Although my talk was during their dinner hour and they had to cut down on eating to attend it, enough students turned up to fill the college theatre with many standing at the back. And in this theatre—although there is no course in drama—they have themselves lately produced *Death of a Salesman, Carousel, Annie Get Your Gun, Finian's Rainbow, Fiorello, Bye, Bye Birdie, Fantasticks,* and, for I was speaking in front of the scenery, *Gideon.* It has had twelve lecturers since September 20th (and we are costly) while there have been ten concerts since October the 16th, including the Rittenhouse Opera Company in *La Bohème.* This doesn't seem to me to be bad going.

One of the tests which we have learned to apply to a virile college is to ask whether any of the students took the trouble to make that march on Washington last summer, protesting against segregation. Many from La Salle did—including a Brother who, I vaguely remember, had the honor to be arrested. I may have remembered wrong—if so, forgive me, Brother Fidelian. I seem to remember asking, What did you do? "Well, we went and bailed him out."

We admired the starched bands or jabots which the Brothers wear. They are called, we were told by the quiet voice of Brother Fidelian, *rabat.* He also told us that one of my books had been read to them by the lector in the refectory of their house of studies, which made me feel pleased. Other gossip was that he had lately been wakened at four in the morning because some gangster was being chased through the campus by the cops (the violent side of America) and that rather a small-sized student had been arrested last week in a snowball riot with the police. La Salle is not coeducational, so it amuses itself by throwing snowballs at policemen instead of capturing female underwear from sororities, as is said to be the case elsewhere.

We had a sunlit journey of it by train both ways. We saw from our morning taxi that the smoothing iron which periodically emits steam as an advertisement in Times Square had an unusual addition to the steam. It had icicles hanging from it. We also noticed that the workmen on the Times Tower building, which is being reconstructed, had all been dressed up as Santa Claus!

Now it is evening and Carol is washing her hair and I am miserable.

I went down to dinner alone and ritually drank a bourbon on the Rocks—my first alcohol in four months—and it was beastly.